I0466932

# THE MORTGAGE EFFECT

## How to Win The Mortgage Game?

It's your turn to #PLAY-THE-GAME

### BOOST YOUR INVESTMENT, YOUR LIFE, YOUR EXCELLENCE

# HAMEED ABDI

## Additional Excellence resources by Hameed Abdi

1. Productivity Excellence (coming Soon)
2. A Players Club (in the works)
3. Hameed Daily - Daily mentoring to Play full out each day - Excellence Everyday
4. Excellence Everyday Journal (limited availability)
5. The Year of Excellence (limited availability)

JOIN OUR CAMPAIGN

JUST DO IT DIFFERENT

Here's to the Ambitious ones, the rebels, troublemakers, The CONTRARY thinkers, THE ACTION TAKERs who DO THINGS DIFFERENTLY.
They HAVE an EXCEPTIONAL VISION.
They EMBRACE EXCELLENCE EVERYDAY, and have no respect for the status quo. You can quote them, disagree with them, glorify or vilify them, but the ONE thing you CANNOT do is TO ignore them! because they change things.
They Impact and Empower Others to achieve financial Freedom.
They PUSH the human race forward. And while some may see them as the IDIOTS, we see genius, because the people who are CRAZY enough to think they can change HUMANITY, are the ones who do.
End
THINK DIFFERENT - DO IT DIFFERENT
EMBRACE EXCELLENCE EVERYDAY

## Praise for the Mortgage Effect

Dear Readers,
Feel free to write your brief praise for the book.
Strongly Encouraged and Humbly requested.

I, personally, love this section (The Mortgage Effect in our Lives). It has a vivid and visual perspective which is great for readers.
**Muskaan Sharma, Writer and Author of Our Broken Realty**

I think this is a guide book that anyone should read before they invest into real estate. This book is making a difference.
A

All in all it's a good reference book.The book is quite detailed for sure. After going through it all I found some items which need your attention.(Those items have added great value in this book. -HA)

**Paramjit S Girn, Fellow Broker**

# THE MORTGAGE EFFECT

## BOOST YOUR INVESTMENT, YOUR LIFE, YOUR EXCELLENCE

### BY HAMEED ABDI

Trusted Mortgage Broker &
President of CARPO Foundation

A portion of every book sold is donated.

Copyright 2024 by Hameed Abdi
Inc.

This book is dedicated to;

**My Mother, My best supporter, The person who sang the song of "YOU CAN WIN IF YOU WANT" in my ears all teenage years.**

خواستن توانستن است. بلی این کتاب را به مادر عزیزم هدیه میکنم. مادری که با خون جان مرا پرورید و اهنگ خواستن توانستن است را در گوش من نجوا کرد.

چون چنین خواهی خدا خواهد چنین
میدهد حق آرزوی متقین
مولانا

با احترام
عمید عمر
ا

Also I dedicate this book to my Father, My biggest inspiration and my role model. I would only be proud, if I could make him proud enough. My father was a Hero.

Wa Salam
Hameed Barya Abdi

And to all those who impacted my life in a positive way!

# Gratitude

Thanks to my Wife Shiwa Omary for all the support,
For reviewing this book and all the small and big
things you do for me and our family. You are the
best I have ever known.
Love,
Hameed

Thanks to the A Team and Shoaib Abdi, my brother
for reviewing this book and the great insights.

**Thanks to all those who reviewed this book pre
release;**
1. Muskan Sharma
2. Paramjit S Girn
3. MAS Khan
4. Sadam Panah
5. Abdullah Meraj
6. Matin Kara
7. Dalia Barsoum
8. Paul Lamoureux
9. Jose Salloum
10. Tricia Gomez

Inspiration

This book is inspired by the works and exemplary leadership of Darren Hardy, Dr. Alireza Azmandian, Dallia Barsoum, Jim Rohn, Tony Robbins, and my mother's intention of writing a book.

Cautions ⚡

The Titles might look simple to you, but Winner's Strategies are no Longer a secret. The secret is that people ignore them because of their simplicity. Simple is excellent. Simple is solid.

You look at this book and you say I already know these, so does everyone else. The secret to higher up is no longer hidden, You know it and everyone else knows it too. But the strategies in this book when applied constantly, slow and steady will win you the race like never before.

After a decade of ups and downs in the Mortgage Industry I have seen it all. Nothing works like the power of the Mortgage Effect if you take simple steps every day and play full out each day - Excellence Everyday and Conquer the Cashflow Game.

Read on and make your life and your investment a masterpiece. Adapt and Thrive to live an "Excellence Everyday" life.

13

The Mortgage Effect

Support Resources


Life and Investment Assessment
Deal Analyzer
Friday Planning System
Association Assessment Game


Gifts from Hameed Abdi;

The complete Audio book of the Mortgage Effect
(coming soon)

A Player's Personal Morning Routine

Access for FREE at;

HameedAbdi.com

IT'S NOT IMPORTANT WHAT YOU LEARN OR NOT LEARN, WHAT STRATEGY YOU USE OR NOT USE. EXCELLENCE COMES FROM THE ACCUMULATED SMALL AND SEEMINGLY INSIGNIFICANT ACTIONS THAT IGNITE THE POWER OF COMPOUND EFFECT WHICH IN YOUR CASE, YOUR COMPOUNDING FACTOR IS YOUR MORTGAGE. MAKE THE MORTGAGE EFFECT WORK FOR YOU EVERY SINGLE DAY AND ACHIEVE EXCELLENCE EVERYDAY.

**EXCELLENCE EVERYDAY**

Introduction

Welcome to The **Mortgage Game** The
wild and cool world of real estate, where, much like
Steve Jobs' vision to dent the universe, the
mortgage game leaves its imprint on our world
every day. The game operates with influence akin
to Jobs' desire to reshape the world, truly making
its mark each day. The game is always changing
with high stakes. We're about to dive into a world of
wonders and reality at the same time that I like to
call "The Mortgage Game" a tale about how
mortgages and real estate prices engage in this
intricate dance that shapes the entire market.

Now, let's break it down. Imagine snagging a
mortgage easily and watching property prices shoot
up like fireworks on New Year's Eve. Suddenly,
owning a home becomes the coolest thing ever, but
it's also a bit tricky. On the flip side, if getting a
mortgage is like trying to solve a Rubik's Cube
blindfolded, well, that usually means real estate
prices take a dip, creating opportunities for savvy
players in the game.

So, in "The Mortgage Game" or as I rather call it
"The Mortgage Effect" we're not just talking about

money and loans; we're talking about a force that can totally shake up the world of real estate. It's like a game where the rules aren't just about dollars and cents; they're about strategy and knowing how to play your cards right.

As we jump into this adventure, let's chat about how mortgages shake up property values. We'll peek into the secret moves that players make to ride the waves, and we'll spill the beans on how the real estate market goes up and down. "The Mortgage Effect" is all about going beyond the usual stuff.

Whether you're a pro investor, a home buyer, or just curious about how housing and real estate works, get ready for a journey into the world of mortgages and real estate. It's like playing a game where "The Mortgage Effect" is your guide through all the twists and turns. Let's kick off this game and see where it takes us!

# The Mortgage Effect in Our Lives

The impact of mortgages extends far beyond financial transactions; it reaches into the very fabric of our lives. "The Mortgage Effect" is not just about numbers and interest rates; it's about dreams taking root, families finding homes, and individuals charting their paths through the landscape of life. So choose wisely. This guide book is here to ensure that the mortgage effect is working in your favor not against us every single time.

Consider the young couple, wide-eyed and hopeful, stepping up their lives and investing into their first home. The mortgage they secure is not just a loan; it is a foundation for their shared future, a place where memories are made,  and a haven they can call their own. The journey of homeownership, shaped by the mortgage they choose, becomes a pivotal chapter in the story of their lives.

For an ambitious entrepreneur, the mortgage is more than a financial arrangement; it's a strategic move. It's the key to unlocking the storefront, the office space, or the workshop that transforms dreams into businesses. The ripple effect of that mortgage decision is felt not only in profit margins, but is in the impact created in communities and industries.

Even for the seasoned investor, navigating the real estate market is a journey with profound effects. The mortgages they maneuver influence not just property portfolios but the dynamics of neighborhoods and the development of entire regions.

"The Mortgage Effect" intertwines with our aspirations, challenges, and triumphs. It guides where we live, the communities we join, and the futures we envision. It's about pursuing stability, seeking growth, and realizing dreams, all woven into the very essence of our lives"

So, as we explore the multifaceted dimensions of mortgages in "The Mortgage Effect", let's not forget that this financial tool transcends the transactional—it has the power to shape the chapters of our lives, leaving a lasting imprint on the stories we tell. In this book we dive into the multiple layers of the Mortgage Effect in the industry. We chase down the ripples, assess the dominos and watch the snow ball of Mortgage and how it SHAPES everything we do. Moreover I recommend to Rinse and Repeat this book Quarterly at least and follow my newsletter daily for better results;

Below shows who scores more for YOU to win the mortgage game; YOU Score 100% when they all score top!

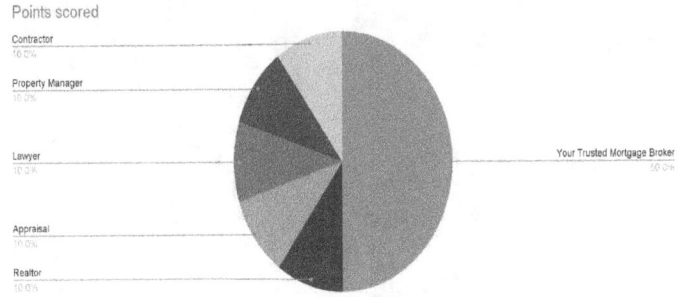

Points scored

Contractor
10.0%

Property Manager
10.0%

Lawyer
10.0%

Appraisal
10.0%

Realtor
10.0%

Your Trusted Mortgage Broker
50.0%

The majority of excellence in the real estate rental business is tied to your level of Utilizing your Knowledge and staying on top of the game by reading. Take action on your reading, RINSE and REPEAT and Action AGain!

# THE MORTGAGE EFFECT

# Chapter One: Rules of the Game

Ever played a game without knowing the rules? It's like navigating through a maze blindfolded. When it comes to mortgages and real estate, understanding the rules is like having a map and a compass. It turns obstacles into opportunities and challenges into victories

Why do we play and what is this game? You know, life's a bit like a game, especially when it comes to mortgages and real estate. It's like having a compass and map - knowing the rules and where the boundaries lie. That's the secret sauce for turning challenges into triumphs and making the best out of any situation.

Now, diving into the game of mortgages is a bit like deciding to go mountain climbing. It's an adventure, and once you're in, there's no turning back midway. No exit signs if you decide to withdraw. So, let's chat about it. We're about to unravel the whole deal in "The Mortgage Effect" by digging into the basic rules of the game.

From the different types of mortgages that are a bit like chess moves to the strategic plays in financing, each chapter is like unlocking a new level. We'll shine a light on the guidelines that can help you turn challenges into victories. Get ready for a journey into the mortgage landscape – it's not just a suggestion, it's the first step towards mastering this complex yet rewarding game. Are you in?

## The Players

Imagine this as our first coffee chat in the world of mortgages. Let's meet the major players —kind of like the main characters in our mortgage story. Ready for some introductions?

Lenders. First up, we have the lenders. Think of them as the wizards who conjure up the funds for your dream home. They come in all shapes and sizes—big banks, credit unions, and online platforms. They set the rules and hold the keys to your mortgage destiny. Each lender has its own flavor and style, adding spice to your mortgage journey"

From your friendly neighborhood bank to the modern online lenders, each one brings its own flavor to the game.

In the mortgage game, lenders are the MVPs, and they come in three categories: A lenders, B lenders, and C lenders.

A Lenders: These are like the rockstars of the mortgage world. They're the A-listers. "A" lenders are the cheapest source of funds, but here's the catch—they're also the strictest. If you're dealing with an A lender, be prepared for high standards. They usually require a credit score above 680 (I normally want my clients to be around 700 just because when you pull the credit it can lower and bit and being on the red line of 680 can become a complication, speaking of experience here), properties that are in tip-top shape, and, in a nutshell, they're the most conservative players in the game. Some examples? Think big banks. They don't mess around.

B Lenders (Alternative Lenders): Now, let's talk about the B team, also known as alternative lenders. These guys are a bit more relaxed and flexible than the A team. Credit unions(sometimes

Credit unions are considered part of the A Lenders, Thanks to Paramjit for correcting me) and trust companies often fit into this category. Ever heard of Home Trust, Equitable Trust, or Effort Trust? Those are some B lenders. Bs are more flexible with things like credit scores—below 600? No problem. They're cool with self-employed folks and properties that might need a bit of TLC. Some A lenders, like Lendwise, even have a B side. If your deal doesn't cut it with the A team, they might just send it over to the B team for consideration if your broker request them to consider approving on the B side like I did one deal with B2B for this long term client very loyal clients "Goliath and David, the deal was approved with B2B bank and all of a sudan Gilaith lost her job midway through the application and then I request B2B to approve the deal on their B side, they approved the same deal on the B side and only wanted the clients to make a larger down payment. Things are flexible with B lenders but they are normally document savvy, they want more documents and more info in order to make sense of your situation to help you out .

Now, there's also the C lenders, the private lenders of anything that is not in A and B. The private lenders have long been unregulated, but recently, there have been some regulations. The key in private lending is the POSITIVE <u>cash flow analysis</u> <u>and return on investment. And for the lenders it's</u> <u>THE EXIT STRATEGY!</u> Private lending is more of a business decision than an emotional home buying decision, so the rules are flexible as long as you have some skin in the game, like a 20% down payment for beginners.

So, when you're playing the mortgage game, knowing your players is key. They're the ones who decide if you get a spot on the mortgage team or if you're sitting this game out.

**Mortgage Insurers:** Now, let's talk about the mortgage insurers. Think of them as the guardians of the game; They're the ones who make sure that lenders aren't left in the lurch if things go south. We'll unravel how they influence the approval process and even play a role in deciding those interest rates.

**Mortgage Brokers:** Next on the list, we've got the RainMakers - The mortgage brokers. These folks are like your personal mortgage GUIDE, connecting you with the right lender. They're in the business of making the game easier for you, negotiating rates, and speaking the language that might otherwise sound like mortgage jargon.

# I am Hameed Abdi

I am a Mortgage Broker. The reason I wrote this book is to prepare you for working with me, my A- Team or any other of my fellow brokers, to win the game and conquer the mortgage mantra. I like to give

back to my community and this is my way of **public service.** My mission is to influence and empower humanity and investors TO Achieve the vision of Positive Financial Freedom. Our A team envisions a Positive Financial Freedom and living a life of **Excellence Everyday**. After almost a decade of Research, Study and practice of Mortgage and real estate in Canada and another decade of service from Afghanistan that included my inspiration and life changing trips to Japan (Small and Medium Enterprises Promotion and Development Program) at age 20 and to india at almost age 19 for learning Research Methodology from the best Researchers at NIRD ( National Institute of Rural Development - India). My Background and my adversity set me up for a great journey in life. I came to Canada almost a decade ago as a Refugee and the first industry I picked an interest in was real estate. Thanks to My cousin and my good friend Matin Kara for introducing me to this amazing world of never ending success(indeed Matin was the reason I came to Canada and did not Stay in the States) and then my Dear Friend Mustafa Nabiyar who hand held me and went above and beyond to make sure I start my career in banking. He even went out of his way and sat down with me to review my resume. More about my journey another time but why I became a broker is because I want to help others build their dreams and make their hopes a reality, like I was able to do because of my **Mother** (my first

teacher) **and my** two Big Brothers
(Munir Abdi and Karim Abdi) they sacrificed
their childhood to be the breadwinner of our
household and make sure we make it to the next
day. Where was your father you asked? Well he
was too busy trying to become the president of
Afghanistan! (Yes this is not a joke, He was damn
serious about it) He was a patriot who was
obsessed with his country and he let go of
everything else for his one thing. (no judgment) I
am still proud of him. He was a HERO.

I am talking about the civil war in the 1990s in
Kabul. My brothers are now here in Canada and I
am proud that I was able to sponsor them after the
recent collapse of the government and withdrawal
of US Troops from Afghanistan. Enough of the past.

Indeed after I sponsored all my five brothers and
my mother with their kids and wives into Canada I
decided to Re-start the CARPO Foundation in
Canada ( A non profit named CARPO that I
founded and brought to fruitation with Nazaar Safi
and Ateeq Shalizi back in 2010 in Kabul)  and NOW
CARPO is proud to sponsor families each year as a
way of giving back to refugees. This is who I am as
a Refugee, I am who came for a better life and I

have decided to go for an Excellence Everyday life! Follow my journey and you will learn more. I am telling you my story not to boast and brag but to impress upon you that a broker is someone who cares about your success and if that's not who I am to you, then you should not be working with me.

I have Professional Connections: Brokers have a network of trusted professionals, including real estate brokers, home inspectors, appraisers, contractors, lawyers, Bankers and so on. I can recommend these experts to ensure you get the best services.

I am Hameed Abdi not because of what I did, but because of all these amazing people in my life who impacted me to excel everyday and DO IT DIFFERENT. LET'S LEAVE OUR MARK!

## Realtors

Let's introduce the role of real estate agents (realtors) in the mortgage journey. They are integral players who help guide buyers through the complex process of finding and purchasing the right property. They are your navigators through the complex  process of finding and purchasing the perfect property. With their market knowledge, negotiation skills, and access to listings, they streamline the buying process, making it less stressful and more efficient

# Real Estate Agents: The Navigators of the Property World

In the intricate world of home buying and financing, real estate agents, often referred to as realtors, are indispensable guides. They serve as the navigators who help you chart a course through the complexities of the property market. Here's why real estate agents are crucial players in the mortgage game:

1. Market Knowledge Experts
2. Negotiation Gurus
3. Access to Listings
4. Paperwork and Legalities
5. Guidance and Support
6. Emotional Support
   - Problem Solvers
   - Local Insights

## The Realtor's Role in the Mortgage Effect

As we explore "The Mortgage Effect", it's clear that real estate agents play a pivotal role in shaping your home buying journey. They do not only help you find the right property,but also ensure that your purchase aligns with your financial and personal goals.

## Why Does It Matters?

- Informed Decisions: With a realtor's expertise, you can make more informed decisions about which property to buy ensuring it's a good fit both financially and personally.
- Efficient Process: Their guidance can streamline the home buying process and make it less stressful and more efficient.
- Better Outcomes: Ultimately, working with a skilled real estate agent can lead to better outcomes, including a favorable purchase price, smooth transactions, and a property that meets your long-term needs.

So, as you journey through the mortgage and home buying process, remember the crucial role of real estate agents. They are your navigators, helping you steer through the complexities of the market and ensuring that you reach your destination smoothly and successfully. Their expertise, support, and network are invaluable assets in the wild world of home financing. amazing, right?

**Just remember, <u>If you are buying for investing work with a specialist realtor who knows real estate investing</u>**

Many realtors claim expertise, but few truly understand the nuances of investment properties. If you are buying a house to live in, choose a realtor you trust. If you trust me, let me introduce you to a realtor I trust.

## Lawyers

It's important to choose a lawyer who will proactively connect with your Mortgage Broker and REaltor to get things moving smoothly for you and not leave everything on you and at the last minute. It's important for you to trust your lawyer and be confident and your mortgage broker and realtor are confident working with them. Not all lawyers are the same and their due diligence  and proactive approach can save your mortgage when it comes to surprises.

**Appraisers**:
Meet the appraisers—the value evaluators. They're the ones who decide the worth of the property. It's like they hold the secret decoder to ensure the mortgage amount aligns with the actual value. These folks play a crucial role in deciding how your mortgage story unfolds.

So, there you have it—the major players in our mortgage adventure. As we dive into "The Mortgage Effect," keep these characters in mind. They're the ones shaping the rules, playing the game, and influencing your journey in the wild world of home financing. Cool, right?

## Bad News

I think Different! I DO DIFFERENT! Yes Like Steve jobs used to do. I am a big fan of his! Unlike other brokers, I give you the bad news first and the good news is always there. However, I  thrive on positivity and I never spread negativity, but bad news is not negative. It's real news! I am Real.

# I am your Trusted Advisor Your GUIDE. YOUR BROKER FOR LIFE. YOU THINK YOU CAN'T take the hard truth? I beg to differ. I ask you to Think Different FOLLOW #THINK_DIFFERENT on Insta for great contents.

## In fact, Steve Jobs' one of the best marketing campaigns was titled "THINK DIFFERENT"

If you're not willing to think differently, the next chapter of creativity might not be for you. This entire book might not be for you. You might as well save some time and read that novel you always do. No offense.

I don't mean to be a Hardy Bardy (self made term) but I feel responsible to be candide as I have embarked on the responsibility of **influencing and empowering you to Positive financial freedom.**

Now, here's the scoop. Unlike those organized sports games where the rules stay put, in the mortgage game, it's like they're doing a midnight dance. Seriously, the rules can change overnight. Picture it: one day you're playing by one set of rules, and the next morning, it's like the game threw you a curveball.

It's kind of like expecting soccer to be soccer every time you step on the field, but in the mortgage game, it's more like waking up and finding out soccer now has an extra set of rules you need to know. Sounds a bit crazy, right?

Now, I want to be upfront with you. There is where I get a little bit of a hard head, I apologize in advance but this is for the good of you and me. If you're not up for this challenge, if the idea of navigating through changing rules isn't your cup of tea, then hey! feel free to close this book. There's no shame in it. You can go back to

renting, **paying off**

# your landlord's mortgage, and let them enjoy the game. No hard feelings! But if you're ready for the challenge, buckle up. We're about to explore the unpredictable yet thrilling world of THE MORTGAGE EFFECT!

## Lender's Hidden Chambers

Now, imagine we're grabbing a coffee and I'm spilling the beans on what really goes on behind the lenders' doors. It's like getting an exclusive pass to the VIP section of the mortgage game – intriguing, right?

A Lenders' Secret Chamber: So, let's step into the secret chamber of A lenders. These are like the rockstars of the mortgage world, think big banks. Behind their doors, it's all about precision and high standards. Credit scores, property conditions, and financial stability – it's like they have a checklist for everything. It's a world where everything needs to be in tip-top shape.

B Lenders' Flex Zone: Now, let's swing by the B lenders' place. This is where credit unions and trust companies hang out. Behind their doors, there's a vibe of flexibility. They're cool with credit scores below 600 and properties that might need a bit of love. It's like a place where adaptability meets opportunity. Need a bit more breathing room? B lenders might just have the solution.

C Lenders' Mystery Room: Lastly, let's sneak into the mystery room of C lenders, or private lenders. Picture it as the backstage pass of the mortgage world. Here, decisions are less tied to strict regulations. It's a bit like a business deal – Cash flow analysis, return on investment – that's the language spoken here. Rules are flexible, especially if you've got some skin in the game, like a hefty down payment.

Thread of Decision: But here's the cool part - behind all these doors, there's a common thread. It's all about weighing risks and rewards. Whether you're in the high-stakes world of A lenders or the flex zone of B lenders, decisions are made based on a dance of risk and reward.

So, as we journey through "The Mortgage Effect," knowing what happens behind these lenders' doors is like having a secret map in the mortgage game. It's your backstage pass to the maneuvers and calculations that shape the decisions in the heart of the mortgage industry. Ready for the insider scoop? Let's roll!

## Where, Who, and What: Lender Landscape

In the world of mortgages, where, who, and what matters. A-space lenders, the rockstars of the mortgage game, often have preferences. Some aren't too keen on lending in areas with less than 25,000 folks. It's like they have their own VIP list for locations. So, where you want to live can impact the game.

Mortgage Wisdom

In the mortgage game, local lenders hold the key. If the big shots aren't backing your play in a specific area, consider teaming up with local credit unions or banks with branches nearby. They know the turf, and

sometimes, going local is your best mortgage strategy in small cute towns.

## Good news, Surprise!

Maybe not so much if you know already. Your Seller Can Be Your Lender. Let's dive into the world of Seller Financing (Vendor Take Back) or **SELLER FINANCING**. I prefer the term Seller financing over Seller Financing and any other term because it has a positive vibe to it and I encourage you to use only this term in your conversation with your sellers cause sometimes you can scare sellers off by using the term Seller Financing cause it is in the name take back. They are sellers and they don't want to take it back. YOU ASK Them to Finance it for you not to take it back! <u>Time for a new term</u>. Any way Seller Financing; It's not your everyday mortgage play, but it could be the unexpected twist that unlocks your homeownership dreams. #SellerFinancingMagic

Seller Financing or "Vendor Take Back," is a type of seller financing in real estate. In a Seller Financing arrangement, the seller of the property acts as the lender or bank, providing financing to the buyer. This can be an alternative to traditional mortgage financing, where a financial institution like a bank provides the loan (this happens a lot in Airbnb and cottages. I was watching Kyle Ford on youtube explaining how he got his Airbnb property in Grand Bend through 100% Seller Financing. If you think it's not possible to do a Seller Financing just go watch his video). In a Seller Financing scenario, the buyer makes payments to the seller over time, and the seller holds a mortgage on the property until the buyer repays the full amount. It's a creative financing option that can benefit both parties under certain circumstances.

# When does SELLER FINANCING Make Sense?

# Seller financing can

make sense in various situations, offering a flexible and creative solution for both buyers and sellers. Here are some scenarios where Seller Financing might be a viable option:

### Buyer's Credit Challenges:

Situation: The buyer has credit challenges and may not qualify for a traditional mortgage.
Seller Financing Solution: The seller acts as the lender, allowing the buyer to make a down payment and pay the remaining purchase price over time. This gives the buyer an opportunity to improve their credit for future refinancing.

### Unique Property Features:

Situation: The property has unique features or challenges that make it less attractive to traditional lenders.
Seller Financing Solution: The seller, having a better understanding of the property, can offer financing to a buyer who sees the potential and is willing to invest in the property.

**Seller's Motivation to Sell Quickly:**
Situation: The seller is motivated to sell quickly and is open to alternative financing arrangements.

Seller Financing Solution: By offering Seller Financing, the seller attracts a broader range of potential buyers, making the property more accessible and potentially speeding up the selling process.

**Market Conditions:**

Situation: In a buyer's market where properties are abundant, sellers may need to offer unique incentives.

Seller Financing Solution: Seller Financing can be a unique selling proposition, especially if other financing options are limited.

**Investment Properties:**

Situation: Buyers interested in investment properties may find it challenging to secure traditional financing for multiple properties.

Seller Financing Solution: Sellers can offer Seller Financing to investors looking to build their portfolio, creating a win-win situation.

**Flexible Terms:**

Situation: Buyers and sellers want flexibility in negotiating terms beyond what traditional lenders may offer.

Seller Financing Solution: Seller Financing allows for more personalized and flexible terms, such as customized interest rates, repayment schedules, and conditions.

It's important for both parties to carefully negotiate and document the terms of a Seller Financing arrangement, considering legal and financial implications. While Seller Financing can be a creative solution, it's not suitable for every situation, and professional advice is important.

# Case Study: A Win-Win with Seller Financing in Real Estate

Scenario: Ciadam, a Turkish immigrant, a homeowner looking to sell her property, found herself in a situation where her home needed substantial repairs and upgrades. On the other hand, Tom, a potential buyer, had credit challenges that made it difficult for him to secure financing from traditional lenders, even from B lenders. Both were in a bit of a bind until they discovered the potential of SELLER financing. Note; you might ask why they don't go to private lenders, seller financing can be cheaper and history has proven that you can borrow with better terms, flexibility and lower cost from sellers because they have an active interest in the deal compared to a third party private lender.

**Challenges:**

1. Property in Need of Repairs:

2. Ciadam's property required significant renovations, and she was hesitant to invest more money before selling.

3. Buyer's Credit Challenges:

- Tom had a credit history that didn't meet the requirements of traditional lenders, making it hard for him to secure a mortgage.

**Seller Financing Solution:**

1. Creative Financing Agreement:

- Ciadam and Tom entered into a SELLER FINANCING agreement where Jane agreed to provide financing for a portion of the property's purchase price.

2. Flexible Repayment Terms:

- The Seller Financing arrangement allowed Tom to make a reasonable down payment and agree to a customized repayment plan over time.

3. Property Improvement Terms:

- To address the property's condition, Ciadam and Tom negotiated terms that allowed Tom to use part of the purchase price for necessary repairs and upgrades.

**Benefits:**

1. Quick Property Sale:

- Ciadam could sell her property faster than if she had waited for extensive renovations, making the property more attractive to a wider range of buyers.
- Access to Homeownership for Tom:
- Tom had the opportunity to become a homeowner despite his credit challenges, with the flexibility to improve his credit over time.

2. Win-Win Negotiation:

- The Seller Financing arrangement created a win-win situation, addressing the unique needs of both the seller and the buyer.

**Conclusion:**

In this case study, SELLER FINANCING emerged as a creative solution that enabled Ciadam to sell her property without immediate investment in renovations. Simultaneously, it provided Tom with an opportunity to achieve homeownership despite his credit challenges. Seller Financing facilitated a mutually beneficial agreement, showcasing the flexibility and creativity that alternative financing options can bring to the real estate market"

## Think of Seller Financing as Your Initial Choice:

So, when it comes to financing, Seller Financing is like your go-to before diving into private options. It's all about having more power in the negotiation game and flexibility. Let me break it down for you:

### Reasoning:
- Basically, the idea here is that Seller Financing is your main squeeze when you're looking at different ways to finance something.

### Leverage:
- When we say "more leverage," we mean you (and the seller) have more say in how things go down with the financing. It's like having a bit more control.

### Negotiating Power and Flexibility:
- Check this out – Seller Financing lets you and the seller talk directly about the deal. That means you can work out terms that fit you both, making it

way more flexible than dealing with a private lender.

**Private Lending Comparison:**

- Just to put it in perspective, Seller Financing is like the cool kid on the block compared to private lending. If you're after terms that work in your favor, Seller Financing might be the way to go.

**Strategic Approach:**

- It's simple: consider Seller Financing first before even thinking about private options. Make it your top choice from the get-go.

**Financial Leverage:**

- When we talk about "more leverage," it means in a Seller Financing setup, you and the seller can shape the financing terms to be a win-win. It's a sweet spot for both parties.

**Implicit Meaning:**

- Read between the lines – in a Seller Financing scenario, you and the seller are in a strong position. You get to set up the financing in a way that's a win for everyone involved.

Remember, whether Seller Financing or private lending makes more sense depends on your specific situation – things like your credit, property condition, and what everyone involved prefers. It's all about finding the right fit.

## Limits on Property Ownership

Some lenders take a conservative approach, capping the number of rental properties they're willing to finance for a single client. This limit often hovers around two rental properties, ensuring a cautious approach to risk.

Total Property Count Matters

On the flip side, other lenders look at the big picture. Instead of focusing solely on rental properties, they consider your entire real estate portfolio, including your primary residence. For these lenders, the magic number is often around five properties. As long as your total property count, both owned and mortgaged, stays within this limit, you're in good standing.

## No Holds Barred

Surprisingly, there are lenders out there with an open-door policy. They don't impose a strict limit on the number of properties you can own. It's a more flexible approach that acknowledges the diverse strategies of real estate investors.

## Navigating the Landscape

When seeking financing, understanding the rules and approaches of different lenders is crucial. Here's how to navigate this complex landscape.

## Strategic Focus: Navigating Financing Beyond Property Limits"

In the intricate world of real estate financing, it's easy to get caught up in the details, especially when it comes to property limits set by lenders. However, here's a secret seasoned investors know – it's not just about the number of properties; it's about strategic focus.

## Beyond Property Limits

While some lenders might have restrictions on the number of properties they finance, it's crucial not to let this become a stumbling block. Instead of worrying about hitting an arbitrary limit, focus on the bigger picture – getting your application approved and securing favorable terms and rates.

Crafting a Strategic Approach

Think of your real estate investments as chess pieces on a board. Craft a financing strategy that not only aligns with your immediate goals but also positions you for future success. Structure your financing in a way that won't hinder your ability to qualify for more properties down the road.

Eye on the Prize: Long-Term Vision

It's easy to be shortsighted, but successful investors keep their eyes on the prize – the long-term vision. Look beyond the immediate constraints, and consider how your financing choices today impact your ability to grow your portfolio tomorrow.

Qualification Flexibility

Opt for lenders who understand the game, those who appreciate your strategic vision. Some lenders are more flexible than others, considering your overall financial health and investment plan rather than fixating on rigid property limits.

Mastering the Financing Game

In the end, real estate financing is a game, and you're the player. Instead of fretting about limits, master the game with strategic focus. Qualify for the properties that matter most to your portfolio. Secure terms and rates that work in your favor. And always keep your eye on the big picture – your long-term vision for real estate success.

# "Unlocking Real Estate Success: The Power of Income"

In the dynamic world of real estate financing, income emerges as the true game-changer. It's not just about the roof over your head; it's about understanding how your income plays a pivotal role in determining the funds a lender is willing to entrust you with.

## Income as the Key

Imagine income as the key that unlocks the door to real estate opportunities. Lenders, much like gatekeepers, evaluate your income to gauge your financial capacity. It's not merely about the amount but the stability and reliability it promises.

## Quantifying Lender Confidence

Your income isn't just a number; it's a symbol of your financial strength. Lenders scrutinize this figure to determine how much they can comfortably lend you. The higher the income, the greater the lender's confidence in your ability to meet financial obligations.

Determining Loan Amounts

When it comes to financing, income is the linchpin. It's the factor that influences not only whether you get the loan but also the magnitude of the loan. A robust and stable income stream can open doors to more significant financial support, enabling you to pursue properties that align with your aspirations.

Building Income Strategies

Strategically building and diversifying your income streams is akin to fortifying your financial castle. Lenders appreciate stability, so showcasing a diversified and reliable income portfolio enhances your standing in the real estate financing game.

Income as a Stepping Stone

Income isn't just a number on your financial statement; it's a stepping stone toward realizing your real estate ambitions. Recognize its significance, leverage its power, and position yourself for success in the intricate world of real estate financing. Your income isn't just key; it's the master key to unlocking the doors to your real estate dreams. Remember the difference between a pond and river when thinking about income and cash. Having a lot of cash is not as good as having a reliable constant income. You need a river not a pond. Think Different!

## "Salary Triumphs: The Lender's Favorite Income"

In the realm of real estate financing, not all incomes are viewed equally by lenders. A reliable, full-time salary is particularly favored because it represents consistent financial stability and predictability, which are key factors for lenders when assessing loan eligibility. While the entrepreneurial spirit thrives on diverse and dynamic income streams, successful entrepreneurs recognize the importance of demonstrating stability. By strategically managing their finances to maintain a regular, dependable salary, they align with lender expectations, combining the best of both entrepreneurial flexibility and financial consistency

Stability and Consistency

Picture this: you, a financial warrior, armed with the steady shield of a full-time salary. Lenders appreciate the stability and consistency that a regular salary brings. It's not just about the amount; it's the predictability that aligns with a lender's quest for financial security.

Favorable Position for Approval

Holding a full-time salary places you in a favorable position with lenders. It signals a committed and steady financial source, akin to a VIP pass in the lending process. This consistent income can expedite loan approvals and potentially grant access to more favorable interest rates, reflecting lenders' increased confidence in your financial management.

Loan Amount Confidence

Your full-time salary isn't just a badge of honor; it's a statement of financial strength. Lenders, much like financial architects, use your salary as a cornerstone in determining the loan amounts they're comfortable offering. The more robust your salary, the greater the financial foundation for your real estate ventures.

Navigating the Lender's Landscape

In the intricate dance of real estate financing, a full-time salary becomes your choreography. It positions you as a trustworthy and committed player, making lenders more willing to join you on the dance floor of property ownership.

Embrace the Salary Advantage

As you navigate the labyrinth of real estate finance, embrace the advantage of a full-time salary. It's not just income; it's a strategic move that places you at the forefront of lender preferences. So, if you're armed with a steady salary, consider it your secret weapon in the pursuit of real estate success.

# "Skin in the Game: The Power of Down Payments"

In the dynamic world of real estate finance, the down payment isn't just a financial transaction; it's your skin in the game, your ticket to the exclusive world of property ownership. Understanding the nuances of down payments is like mastering a strategic move in the grand chessboard of real estate.

# Zero Down: A Tempting Mirage

Imagine stepping into homeownership without an upfront payment. Zero-down options, like cashback mortgages for primary residences, offer this enticing illusion. However, these options are mostly restricted and increasingly rare, especially as federal regulations now limit such products through big banks and A lenders. Alternative strategies, like combining Vendor Take-Backs (Seller Financings) with loans from A or B lenders, still provide creative pathways for those looking to minimize initial cash outlay. Later in this book, (your mortgage guide), we'll explore some of these innovative options

### 5% Down: The Gateway to Your Home

For your primary residence, a down payment of 5% is the golden key. It opens the door to homeownership, allowing you to step into the sanctuary of your own space. This modest down payment option provides a pathway for those eager to escape the cycle of renting and embrace the joys of property ownership.

## Zero Down around the World

Several countries offer zero down payment options for home buyers, often as part of initiatives to make homeownership more accessible. Here is a brief synopsis of a few notable countries:

### United States

In the U.S., zero down payment home loans are available through specific government-backed programs such as:

1. **VA Loans**: Available to veterans, active-duty service members, and certain members of the National Guard and Reserves. These loans are provided by private lenders but backed by the Department of Veterans Affairs, requiring no down payment or private mortgage insurance (PMI).
2. **USDA Loans**: Offered through the U.S. Department of Agriculture, these loans are designed for rural and suburban homebuyers. They also require no down payment and have flexible credit requirements.

## Canada

In Canada, zero down payment mortgages are generally not available due to stricter regulations following the 2008 financial crisis. However, some programs allow for alternative solutions:

1. **Cash Back Mortgages**: Some lenders offer cash back mortgages where a certain percentage of the mortgage amount is given back to the borrower at closing, which can be used as a down payment.

## Australia

In Australia, zero down payment options are limited, but there are a few pathways:

1. **First Home Loan Deposit Scheme (FHLDS)**: Allows first-time home buyers to purchase a property with as little as 5% deposit, with the government guaranteeing the loan, thus reducing the need for lenders' mortgage insurance.

## United Kingdom

In the UK, there are several schemes aimed at helping first-time buyers:

1. **Help to Buy**: This government-backed scheme allows buyers to purchase a new-build home with a 5% deposit. The government provides an equity loan of up to 20% (40% in London) of the property's value.

## Singapore

In Singapore, the Housing and Development Board (HDB) provides several assistance schemes for first-time buyers:

1. **HDB Loans**: Eligible first-time buyers can get an HDB loan with a down payment as low as 10% of the purchase price, and for those purchasing resale flats, various grants can effectively reduce the initial cash outlay.

## Summary

Zero down payment home buying options are primarily available in the United States, with notable programs like VA and USDA loans. Other countries like Canada, Australia, the UK, and Singapore offer various schemes and support to lower the initial financial barrier to homeownership, though they may not be explicitly zero down payment. These initiatives aim to make homeownership more accessible, particularly for first-time buyers and specific eligible groups.

## 20% Down: The Investment Threshold

Now, if your real estate aspirations extend to the world of rental investments, the game changes. A down payment of 20% becomes the standard, the threshold you must cross to unlock the potential of income-generating properties. This isn't just a financial commitment; it's your stake in the realm of real estate entrepreneurship.

## The Essence of Skin in the Game

Why do down payments matter? Because they signify your commitment, your skin in the game. Whether it's the modest 5% for a cherished home or the substantial 20% for an investment venture, your down payment is the tangible expression of your dedication to the journey of property ownership.

**Navigating the Landscape**

As you navigate the diverse landscapes of real estate, understand the power of your down payment. It's not just a financial prerequisite; it's your declaration that you're ready to invest, to build, and to thrive in the world of property ownership. So, embrace the concept of skin in the game, for it is the foundation upon which your real estate dreams will flourish.

# Documenting Your Financial Identity: A Checklist for Full-Time Salaried Applicants"

Embarking on the mortgage journey as a full-time salaried applicant? Congratulations on taking the first step toward homeownership! To ensure a smooth sailing experience, let's unpack the essential documents you'll need to present. Think of it as your financial dossier, providing lenders with a comprehensive view of your financial identity.

Proof of Income: The Crown Jewel

- Recent pay stubs: A snapshot of your consistent income.
- Employment verification letter: A formal confirmation of your full-time status.

Tax Documents: A Glimpse into Your Financial History

- Tax Return (T1 General and other forms): Offering insights into your annual income.
- Notice of Assessment: A document from the tax authorities (CRA) verifying your filed taxes.

Financial Snapshot: Bank Statements (normally three months)

- Recent bank statements: Providing a glimpse of your financial transactions and stability.

Credit Health: Your Credit Report

- Credit report: A comprehensive record of your credit history and score.
- Explanation for any derogatory items: If applicable, provide context for any negative entries.

Identity Verification: Government Issued ID

- Driver's license or passport: Confirming your identity.

Residence History: Where You've Called Home

- Rental payment history: If renting, showcasing your payment consistency.
- Proof of residence: Confirming your current living situation.

Debt Obligations: The Full Picture
- Details of existing loans or debts: Providing clarity on your financial obligations.

Employment Stability: Confirmation of Your Career Path
- Employment history: An overview of your professional journey.

Letter of Employment: A Formal Introduction
- Letter from your employer: Introducing you, your role, and your income.

Down Payment Source: A Paper Trail
- Proof of down payment: Documenting the source of your down payment funds.

Gift Letter (if applicable): When Loved Ones Contribute
- If receiving a gift, a letter from the giver: Confirming the nature of the gift.

Tips for Success:
- Ensure all documents are up-to-date and within the specified time frames.
- Communicate proactively with your broker if there are any unique circumstances or challenges.

By assembling this comprehensive set of documents, you're not just meeting the lender's requirements; you're crafting a compelling narrative of your financial stability and readiness for homeownership. So, gather your documents, embark on this exciting journey, and let the story of your homeownership unfold!

## "Navigating the Mortgage Maze: Documenting Income for Part-Time Applicants"

Exploring homeownership as a part-time worker? Many lenders understand and accommodate the evolving nature of employment. Here's a breakdown of the key documents you'll need to illustrate your income and financial standing

Income Verification: Demonstrating Part-Time Earnings
- Recent pay stubs: Reflecting your part-time income over a specific period.

- Employment verification letter: Confirming your part-time status and role responsibilities.

Tax Documents: Painting Your Financial Picture
- Two Recent years T1 General tax return: Offering a glimpse of your annual income from all sources.
- Two Recent years Notice of Assessment: A document from tax authorities validating your filed taxes.

3 months Bank Statements: A Peek into Financial Stability
- Recent bank statements: Illustrating your financial transactions and stability.

Consent to obtain Credit Report: Your Credit Health Snapshot
- Credit report: A detailed record of your credit history and score.
- Explanation for any derogatory items: Providing context for negative entries, if applicable.

Identity Confirmation: two Government Issued ID
- Driver's license or passport: Validating your identity.

Residence Confirmation: Where You Call Home
- Rental payment history: If renting, showcasing your payment consistency.

- Proof of residence: Confirming your current living situation.

Debt Overview: A Clear Financial Landscape
- Details of existing loans or debts: Outlining your financial obligations.

Employment History: Showcasing Stability
- Employment history: Providing an overview of your professional journey.

Letter of Employment: Presenting Your Work Profile
- Letter from your employer: Introducing you, your role, and your part-time income.

Down Payment Source: Documenting Your Investment
- Proof of down payment: Detailing the source of your down payment funds.

Gift Letter (if applicable): When Loved Ones Contribute
- If receiving a gift, a letter from the giver: Confirming the nature of the gift.

Tips for Success:
- Keep your documents up-to-date and within the specified time frames. Normally 30 days
- Proactively communicate with your lender about any unique circumstances.

As you compile this collection of documents, remember that each piece contributes to your story of financial stability and readiness for homeownership. Part-time employment is a valid and recognized source of income, and by presenting a clear financial picture, you're paving the way for a successful mortgage application journey. Happy documenting!

## Decoding Self-Employed Income for Mortgage Magic

Welcome to the realm of self-employed income in the mortgage game! If you're your own boss, whether as a sole proprietor, rocking your personal legal name, or steering a corporation, you're in for a unique ride. Here's the inside scoop on how to dazzle lenders and turn your self-employed status into a mortgage triumph.

**Credit Score Showtime:**

Picture your credit score as the spotlight in a blockbuster film. For self-employed individuals, it's your time to shine. Lenders love a robust credit score—it's like having the hero's journey in your financial tale. So, keep it strong, and you'll be the star of your mortgage application.

**Tax Returns: Your Financial Script:**

Think of your tax returns as the script that tells your financial story. Lenders dive into this narrative to understand your income, deductions, and overall financial plot twists. So, make sure your tax returns are a compelling tale that showcases your financial stability.

**Line 15000: The Star of the Show:**

In the tax return saga, Line 15000 of your Notice of Assessment is the undeniable star. This magical line consolidates your financial performance into a single act. Lenders look at it with awe and reverence, as it holds the key to understanding your income dynamics.

**The Two-Year Income Average:**

Now, here's where the plot thickens. Lenders often take a cinematic approach by averaging your income over two years. It's like ensuring your financial story isn't a one-hit wonder but a consistent chart-topper. This method aligns self-employed individuals with the familiar terrain of salaried employees.

**Lights, Camera, Financial Action:**

Successfully navigating the self-employed income scene requires a bit of financial choreography. Ensure your tax returns and financial documents are a well-rehearsed dance that showcases a stable and healthy income stream. It's not about smoke and mirrors; it's about presenting yourself as a reliable financial lead in the eyes of lenders.

So, whether you're a solopreneur or the captain of your corporate ship, understanding the nuances of self-employed income sets the stage for mortgage success. Consider this your backstage pass to the inner workings of self-employed finances in the mortgage world—because when you know the script, you're ready for your starring role! Let's make your self-employed journey in the mortgage game an Oscar-worthy performance.

# Navigating Stated Income: A Broker's Perspective

In the intricate dance of mortgage applications, stated income emerges as a crucial note. Your mortgage broker, akin to a skilled choreographer, holds the expertise to guide you through this intricate routine. Here's how they orchestrate the ballet of stated income:

**Gross Income Evaluation**

Your broker, armed with financial acumen, assesses your gross income. This initial step involves understanding the total income before deductions. It serves as the foundational note in composing your stated income.

**Industry Dynamics**

Every profession carries its unique financial melody. Your broker, well-versed in industry intricacies, aligns your stated income with the rhythm of your specific field. This ensures that your declaration harmonizes with the established standards of your profession.

**Bank Statements as Crescendo**

The recent 6 months of your financial history, encapsulated in bank statements, serves as the crescendo in this symphony. Your broker delves into these documents, examining the ebb and flow of your finances. This not only validates the consistency of your income but also contributes to the plausibility of your stated amount.

**Reasonable Determination**

Armed with insights into your gross income, industry benchmarks, and bank statements, your broker embarks on the task of reasonable determination. This involves strategically arriving at a stated income figure that reflects your financial reality without deviating into the realm of exaggeration.

**Risk Mitigation Strategies**

Brokers, akin to skilled conductors, are adept at minimizing risks. They employ strategies to present your stated income in a way that aligns with lender expectations, reducing potential skepticism. This might involve additional documentation or nuanced explanations to fortify the narrative.

**Ensuring Compliance**

In the intricate symphony of mortgage regulations, compliance is the key refrain. Your broker ensures that your stated income adheres to the rules governing mortgage applications. This meticulous attention to compliance enhances the credibility of your financial composition.

**Customized Approach**

Recognizing that each financial melody is unique, your broker crafts a customized approach. They consider your individual circumstances, industry nuances, and financial history, ensuring that your stated income is a tailored composition that resonates with lenders.

**Transparent Communication**

Effective communication is the melody that ties the symphony together. Your broker engages in transparent communication, keeping you in tune with the process. They explain the rationale behind the determined stated income, fostering a collaborative approach in the journey.

Entrust your stated income to the skilled hands of your mortgage broker. With their expertise, they transform the potentially complex composition into a harmonious arrangement that elevates your mortgage application, ensuring it strikes the right chords with lenders.

## Documents for self employed applications

Navigating the terrain of a mortgage application as a self-employed individual requires a curated ensemble of documents to present a comprehensive financial profile. Here's your checklist for a harmonious mortgage application:

**Personal Identification:**

- 2 Government-issued photo IDs (e.g., driver's license, Permanent residence card or passport).

**Proof of Business Registration:**
- Business license or registration documents.
- Articles of Incorporation (for corporations).

**Business Financials:**
- Business bank statements (typically the last 6 to 12 months).
- 2 Previous years' complete financial statements (if applicable).

**Personal Tax Documents:**
- Notice of Assessment (NOA) for the past two years.
- T1 General tax returns for the past two years.
- If incorporated, T2 Corporate tax returns.

**Proof of Income:**
- Six months of personal bank statements.
- Invoices or contracts that validate income.

**Credit Report:**

- A consent to pull a Personal credit report.

**Proof of Down Payment:**
- Bank statements illustrating the source of your down payment.

**Property Information (If Identified):**
- Details of the property you intend to purchase. (MLS and APS)

**Debt Information:**
- Any outstanding debts or liabilities.

**Legal Documentation (If Applicable):**
- Shareholder agreements (for corporations).
- Partnership agreements (for partnerships).

**Other Financial Assets:**
- Investment statements.
- RRSP or pension statements.

**Business Structure Clarification:**
- Explanation of the nature of your business, especially if it involves specialized industries or unique revenue streams.

Remember, the key to a successful mortgage application lies in the clarity and completeness of your documentation. Providing a detailed and organized set of documents enhances your broker's ability to present your financial composition convincingly to lenders. It's your symphony, and each document plays a crucial note in composing the melody of your mortgage application.

## Decision time

Solve the dilemma of a self employed corporation owner to pay himself or not in order to have a higher income on his personal tax return line 15000?

The decision on whether a self-employed corporation owner should pay themselves or not involves a delicate balance between managing personal income for mortgage qualification and optimizing the financial health of the business. Here's a breakdown of considerations:

**Paying Yourself:**

    **Pros:**

- **Higher Income on Line 15000:** Paying yourself a reasonable salary increases the income reported on Line 15000 of your personal tax return, which is a key factor considered by A lenders.
- **Stability for Mortgage Approval:** Regular income can contribute to a stable financial profile, enhancing your chances of mortgage approval.

**Cons:**
- **Tax Implications:** Personal income is subject to personal income tax. Ensure that the salary aligns with your overall tax strategy and minimizes tax liability.

**Not Paying Yourself:**

**Pros:**
- **Business Growth:** Retaining profits within the corporation allows for potential business expansion, investment, or debt reduction.
- **Tax Deferral:** Corporate income is typically taxed at a lower rate than

personal income, providing tax deferral benefits.

**Cons:**

- **Lower Line 15000 Income:** Lenders primarily focus on Line 15000 income for mortgage approval. A lower reported income may impact your ability to qualify for the desired mortgage amount.

**Balancing Act:**

**Reasonable Salary:** If you opt to pay yourself, ensure that the salary is reasonable and aligns with industry standards. This involves assessing your role, responsibilities, and industry benchmarks.

**Tax Planning:** Consult with a tax professional to develop a tax-efficient strategy. This may involve a combination of salary, dividends, and other tax-saving measures.

**Mortgage Broker Insight:** Consider how ambitious your real estate portfolio building is? If you are aggressively looking to add more properties and the profit that you will gain from buying more houses is going to

<u>offset the loss in the taxes paid due to the reported income then go for it and if not consider not reporting and opt into going for a "B" lender and utilizing an stated income program or other alternatives. Again it comes down to your plan.</u>

Ultimately, the decision should align with both personal and business financial goals. Striking a balance between optimizing personal income for mortgage qualification and fostering business growth is key. Professional advice from both tax and mortgage perspectives can provide valuable insights tailored to your specific situation.

## Case Study: Unlocking Opportunities with Stated Income Program

**Meet Alex, a seasoned real estate investor who operates under a corporation.** Despite strong corporate finances, Alex's personal tax return showed lower income. His objective? Acquiring another property to expand his portfolio. **Alex had an impressive credit score and a successful**

portfolio of rental properties. His goal? Acquiring another property to expand his real estate portfolio.

**Challenges Faced:**

- **Declined by Bank:** Alex approached his primary bank, hoping to leverage the strong financial standing of his corporation. However, the bank, adhering to strict income verification criteria, declined his mortgage application based on his personal tax return.

**Turning to Alternatives:**

- **Credit Union's Stated Income Program:** Alex's Undeterred broker, explored alternative options and found a credit union offering a stated income program. Unlike traditional lenders, the credit union considered his corporation's robust income without solely relying on his personal tax return.

**Key Highlights:**

**Stated Income Advantage:** The credit union's stated income program allowed Alex to showcase his corporation's actual income, enabling him to qualify for the mortgage despite the disparity in his personal income. **Credit Score Strength:** Alex's stellar credit score played a crucial role. The credit union, recognizing his creditworthiness, was more inclined to extend favorable terms despite the unconventional income structure. **Down Payment and Terms:** the downside is that Alex needed to pay a 25% down payment, the credit union provided a mortgage with a 25-year amortization period.

**Outcome:**

- **Successful Property Acquisition:** With the credit union's support, Alex successfully acquired the additional property, adding another gem to his real estate portfolio.

**Key Takeaways:**

- **Stated Income Programs:** For individuals with strong corporate income and lower personal income, exploring lenders with stated income programs can open doors to financing opportunities.

- **Credit Score Matters:** A robust credit score can serve as a valuable asset, influencing lenders to consider unconventional income structures more favorably.
- **Flexibility in Terms:** Alternative lenders, such as credit unions, may offer more flexible terms, allowing investors like Alex to tailor financing to their unique needs.

This case illustrates how diversifying financing options and considering lenders with specialized programs can turn challenges into opportunities, ultimately fueling real estate investment success.

## Navigating Mortgage Challenges with Commission Income

For individuals relying on commission income, securing a mortgage comes with its own set of considerations. Unlike those eligible for stated income programs, commission-based earners face unique challenges. Let's explore how lenders typically assess commission income and what potential applicants should keep in mind.

**Understanding Commission Income Challenges:**

- **Ineligibility for Stated Income Programs:** Unfortunately, commission-based earners typically do not qualify for stated income programs.
- **Income Assessment:** Lenders scrutinize commission income by reviewing the Notice of Assessment (NOA), specifically focusing on line 15000, which represents the total income. However, relying on commission income poses challenges, as it can vary significantly from year to year.

**Lender Practices for Commission Income:**

- **Two-Year Average:** To mitigate the impact of income fluctuations, lenders often calculate an average of the commission income over the past two years. This provides a more stable representation of the borrower's earning capacity.

**Key Considerations for Commission Earners:**

**Documenting Income Stability:** Strengthen your application by demonstrating a consistent income stream. Additional documentation like employment contracts or client agreements can clarify income predictability.

**Tax Planning Impact:** Consider how tax-saving measures that reduce reported income can impact your mortgage eligibility.

**Building Strong Credit:** Maintaining a solid credit score is crucial, enhancing credibility and potentially offsetting income variability challenges

## Case-by-Case Evaluation:

Each commission-based mortgage application undergoes a case-by-case evaluation. Lenders consider various factors, including the applicant's creditworthiness, overall financial health, and the stability of the commission income.

## Conclusion:

While commission income introduces complexities to the mortgage application process, proactive measures can enhance eligibility. Commission earners should work on showcasing income stability, maintaining a solid credit profile, and understanding how lenders assess their unique financial circumstances. By addressing these considerations, individuals relying on commission income can navigate the mortgage landscape more effectively.

Commissioned income applicants like **realtors** and others are considered self employed for the sake of the documentation required thus they provide the same as self employed with an additional letter from their company for example for a realtor a letter from the brokerage and their license copy.

## Unlocking Mortgage Opportunities for Cash Income Applicants with B Lenders

In the realm of mortgage financing, cash income applicants often find solace in the flexibility offered by B lenders. These financial institutions, specializing in alternative lending, recognize the unique circumstances of individuals relying on cash income. Let's unravel the key considerations and opportunities for cash income applicants exploring options with B lenders.

**B Lenders' Perspective on Cash Income:**

**Document Flexibility:** B lenders, in contrast to their more conservative A lender counterparts, are often more flexible in accepting alternative forms of income documentation. This proves beneficial for cash income earners who may not have conventional pay stubs or tax records.

**Industry Norms and Business Licenses:** B lenders consider industry norms and professional certifications. Cash income applicants, such as freelance hair stylists or babysitters with valid licenses, can leverage their business credentials to substantiate their income claims.

**Proving Income with B Lenders:**

**Invoices and Client Letters:** Cash income applicants can provide invoices and letters from clients attesting to the consistency and reliability of their earnings. This personalized documentation adds a layer of authenticity to the income verification process.

**Business License Validation:** Having a valid business license strengthens the credibility of the cash income source. B lenders often acknowledge and accept these licenses as proof of a legitimate income-generating venture.

**Down Payment Considerations:**

**Minimum 20% Down Payment:** While B lenders offer more flexibility, cash income applicants typically need to make a minimum down payment of 20%. This requirement demonstrates commitment and reduces perceived risk for the lender.

**Case-by-Case Variability:** B lenders approach each case individually, considering the unique circumstances of the applicant. While a 20% down payment is a standard guideline, B lenders may adjust requirements based on the overall financial picture presented by the applicant.

**Conclusion:**

Cash income applicants should not be deterred by the challenges posed by conventional lenders. B lenders, recognizing the diversity of income sources, offer viable solutions for those relying on cash earnings. By strategically leveraging industry norms, business licenses, and personalized documentation, cash income applicants can access mortgage opportunities with B lenders, bringing them one step closer to their homeownership goals.

## Mortgage Requirements for New Immigrants

Welcome to the land of opportunity! As a new immigrant as I once was and still kinda I am, navigating the mortgage game may seem like entering uncharted territory, but fear not—I am here to guide you through the process and ensure you're well-equipped for success.

### Establishing Credit History

One of the key aspects lenders look at is your credit history. For new immigrants, building a credit history in your new home can be a challenge. But worry not—there are strategies to showcase your financial responsibility. Opening a local bank account, obtaining a secured credit card, and paying bills on time are great ways to start building that credit profile.

## Employment Stability

Lenders often prefer borrowers with a stable employment history. As a new immigrant, showcasing your job stability and providing proof of employment will work in your favor. Employment contracts, pay stubs, or a letter from your employer can strengthen your mortgage application.

## Down Payment Requirements

The down payment is your skin in the game, and different lenders may have varying requirements. New immigrants might face unique considerations, and the down payment could range from 5% to 20%, depending on the lender and your financial situation. Exploring down payment assistance programs or grants could also be beneficial. The only way to pay the minimum down payment is if you have a full time job and provide alternative credit like bank letters or landlord letters plus an international credit report if possible.

**Simply put; It's a** Varying Requirements situation: Down payments for new immigrants can range from 5% to 20%, depending on your financial situation and the lender's policies. Explore down payment assistance programs in your city if available.

## Documents

Lenders will be looking for a letter of reference from your homebank and transfer of your credit report/history if available in addition to a statement of net worth. Don't mix this up with new immigrants who have been in Canada for at least one year and have established some credit. Those types of newcomers can actually get a normal mortgage provided they have a solid salaried income. Like Manpreet Singh who is an accountant who moved from India to work in one of Linamar plants in Guelph, Ontario. He qualifies in the first six months to buy a home providing his credit is in good standing.

Or Cumali another Turkish Newcomer who has been sponsored through LMIA by his employer and he is a skilled Carpenter so from day one in Canada he has a pay cheque and he starts to earn money. The only thing I had to advise him to do was to get two credit accounts and keep using them responsibly (pay on time) and reasonably (40% of Limit) to build credit and by end of year one he was ready to buy a house with minimum down payment.

# Permanent Residency Status

Important Update: Prohibition on Non-Canadian Purchase of Residential Property in Canada

As of January 1, 2023, the Prohibition on the Purchase of Residential Property by Non-Canadians Act ("the Act") is in effect, imposing restrictions on non-Canadian individuals from acquiring residential property in Canada for a duration of two years.

**Key Highlights:**

### Definition of Residential Property:

- The Act categorizes residential property as buildings containing three dwelling units or less, encompassing semi-detached houses and condominium units.
- Notably, the Act does not restrict the purchase of larger buildings with four or more dwelling units.

### Exemptions for Non-Canadians:

- Non-Canadians are permitted to acquire residential properties located outside of Census Metropolitan Areas (CMA) and Census Agglomerations (CA).

### Exceptions in Defined Circumstances:

- Certain exceptions exist, allowing non-Canadians to purchase residential property under specific circumstances.

**Here is a summary of the ban and what an investor still can do, Looking on the positive side;**

**Despite the ban, investors can still:**

1. Purchase properties outside of Census Metropolitan Areas (CMAs) or Census Agglomerations (CAs), as defined by Statistics Canada's geographical classifications. For detailed geographic classifications, refer to the CMHC map application.
2. Temporary residents studying in Canada can invest in property if they meet specific criteria, including enrollment in a designated institution, tax filings, physical presence, first-time home purchase, and a price limit of $500,000.
3. Temporary residents working in Canada with a valid work permit and at least 183 days of validity remaining can also buy property if they have not previously purchased a residential property.
4. Refugees who have been granted protection or are considered protected persons under the Immigration and Refugee Protection Act are eligible to purchase property.
5. Refugee claimants and individuals fleeing international crises can invest in property if they have eligible claims or temporary resident status for humanitarian reasons.
6. Accredited members of foreign missions holding valid diplomatic passports can purchase property in Canada.
7. Non-Canadian spouses and common-law partners can invest in property together with their Canadian or eligible non-Canadian partner.
8. Indigenous people and communities can purchase property if the prohibition conflicts with their rights recognized under Section 35 of the Constitution Act, 1982.

## Summary and Next Steps:

**Navigating the Ban Positively:**

- **Explore Alternative Locations:** Focus on regions outside the restricted areas to find potential investment opportunities.
- **Leverage Exemptions:** Utilize the exemptions available based on your specific status and circumstances.
- **Stay Updated:** Regulations can change, so keeping abreast of the latest updates is crucial. You can stay informed by checking the CMHC map application for detailed geographic classifications and the most recent information on the regulations.

## Need More Information?

**Get in Touch:** For a comprehensive guide on foreign investment and detailed advice tailored to your situation, reach out to me or the A-Team at Hameed@HameedAbdi.com

**Online Resources:** Use the CMHC's resource on the Prohibition Act to explore current regulations and stay updated on amendments

**USEFUL LINK;**

**<u>Request the link. Email.</u>**

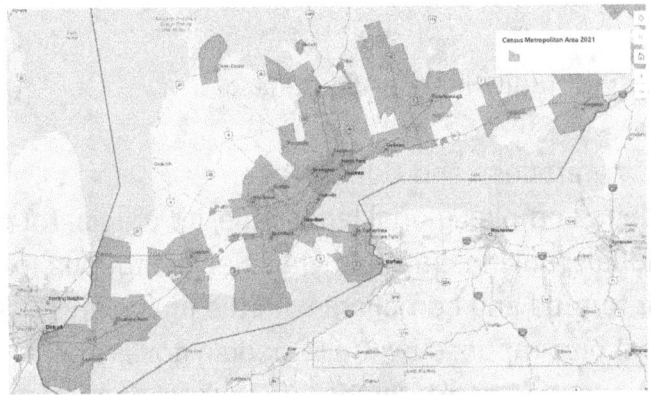

As of now June 11 2024, Foreign investors can buy anything that is not marked green on the above map.

Stay informed and navigate the regulations effectively by accessing the provided links or by searching for "CMHC Non-Canadian Purchase of Property" online. It's crucial to stay updated on any amendments or changes to ensure compliance with current regulations.

# Sanctions

Caution for Individuals and Entities:

- Awareness and Compliance:

In today's complex global landscape, it's crucial for individuals, businesses, and financial institutions to stay informed and compliant with the financial prohibitions imposed by the Canadian government. These sanctions are vital tools in maintaining national security and upholding international law.

- Staying Informed:

Regularly updating yourself on changes to sanction lists and seeking legal advice is essential to avoid unintended legal consequences. The Canadian government provides comprehensive resources and lists detailing current sanctions, including financial prohibitions.

- Accessing Official Information:

For the most accurate and current information, consult official government websites such as Global Affairs Canada. These resources offer detailed insights into the nature and scope of various sanctions, helping you navigate compliance effectively.

**Building Strong Relationships with Mortgage Brokers: Your Key to Navigating Lending Rules**

In the dynamic landscape of lending, staying informed and making the right financial decisions can be a challenging task. However, there's a secret weapon that can make this journey smoother and more successful: building a strong relationship with a Mortgage Broker as your **trusted advisor.**

**Why Choose a Mortgage Broker?**

**Expertise in Lending Rules:**
- Mortgage Advisors are professionals who specialize in the mortgage industry. They have in-depth knowledge of lending rules, regulations, and a broad understanding of <u>various financial products</u>.

**Continuous Updates:**
- Lending rules and products often undergo changes. A Mortgage Broker

stays consistently updated on these changes, ensuring that you receive the most current and relevant information.

**Personalized Guidance:**

- Every financial situation is unique. A Mortgage Broker provides personalized guidance based on your specific needs, goals, and financial profile.

**Access to Diverse Products:**

- Mortgage Brokers work with a variety of lenders and have access to diverse mortgage products. This allows them to find the best solutions tailored to your requirements.

**Navigating Challenges:**

- Financial landscapes can be complex, and unexpected challenges may arise. Mortgage Brokers offer support in navigating hurdles, finding solutions, and making the lending process smoother.

**How to Build a Strong Relationship?**

Communicate, Check in, Build trust.

**Open Communication:**

- Communicate openly about your financial goals, concerns, and any changes in your circumstances. This helps the Mortgage Advisor tailor their guidance to your evolving needs.

**Regular Check-Ins:**

- Schedule regular check-ins with your Mortgage Advisor, especially if there are significant life changes or if you're considering new financial ventures. This ensures that your mortgage strategy aligns with your current situation.

**Trust and Transparency:**

- Trust is the foundation of a strong relationship. Be transparent about your financial situation, and trust your Mortgage Advisor to provide the best advice for your unique circumstances.

**Ask Questions:**

- Don't hesitate to ask questions about lending rules, mortgage products, or any aspect of the process that you find unclear. A good Mortgage Advisor will take the time to ensure you fully understand your options.

**Long-Term Partnership:**

- Consider your relationship with a Mortgage Broker as a long-term partnership. As your financial goals evolve, having a trusted advisor by your side ensures continuity in making well-informed decisions.

  I pride myself for being your broker for life! Understand this that if you are not considering me your broker for life you should not be working with me so is the same for any other broker that you choose to work with. Find your broker for life. I value loyalty greatly and as Harvey say's in my favorite netflix show; Suits and I quote " Loyalty is a two way street" what show you say; If you have not watched it yet! You are missing out on something great. Do yourself a favor and get some bench watching time. "Suits" is worth it.

Building a strong relationship with a Mortgage Broker is your key to navigating the intricate world of lending rules. It's an investment in your financial well-being, providing you with the guidance and support needed to achieve your homeownership and investment dreams.

## Unlocking Your Borrowing Potential: Understanding Debt Coverage Ratios

When it comes to securing a mortgage, understanding how much you can borrow is a crucial piece of the puzzle. Enter the world of debt coverage ratios, specifically the Gross Debt Servicing Ratio (GDSR).

Gross Debt Servicing Ratio (GDSR): Decoding Your Borrowing Capacity

**What is GDSR?**

Also referred to as GDS for short. The GDSR is a financial metric that lenders use to assess your ability to cover housing-related expenses. It takes into account the proportion of your income needed to cover your mortgage, property taxes, heating costs, and 50% of condo fees (if applicable).

How is GDSR Calculated?

The formula is simple:

$$GDSR = \left( \frac{MortgagePayment + PropertyTaxes + HeatingCosts}{GrossAnnualIncome} \right) \times 100$$

Understanding the Components:

> Mortgage Payment: This includes both principal and interest.
> Property Taxes: The annual property tax associated with the property you're considering.
> Heating Costs: An estimate of the annual heating expenses for the property.

What Does GDSR Tell You?

GDSR provides a percentage representing the portion of your income needed to cover housing-related expenses. Lenders typically have a maximum allowable GDSR, often around 32% for 'A' lenders and up to 48% for 'B' lenders, though this can vary

Debt Load and Borrowing Capacity:

Optimal GDSR: Aim for a GDSR below the lender's maximum to ensure flexibility in your budget and financial stability.
Impact on Borrowing Capacity: A higher GDSR may limit your borrowing capacity. Managing and optimizing GDSR can enhance your eligibility for a mortgage.

Key Takeaways:

- Budget Prudently: Understanding your GDSR helps you budget for homeownership responsibly.
- Lender Criteria: Different lenders may have varying GDSR thresholds; explore options to find a suitable fit.
- Holistic Financial Picture: GDSR is part of the broader financial assessment; consider other debt obligations for a comprehensive view.

**Total Debt Servicing Ratio (TDSR):**

**What is TDSR?**

TDS for short. TDSR is a financial indicator that assesses your ability to manage all your debts, not just housing-related expenses. It considers all your monthly debt obligations in relation to your income.

### Calculating TDSR: The Formula

$$TDSR = (MortgagePayment + PropertyTaxes + HeatingCosts + Other\ DebtPayments\ /\ GrossAnnualIncome) \times 100$$

### Key Components:

**Mortgage Payment:** This encompasses both principal and interest.
**Property Taxes:** Annual property tax associated with the property.
**Heating Costs:** An estimate of annual heating expenses for the property.
**Other Debt Payments:** Includes payments for loans, credit cards, and other outstanding debts.

### Understanding TDSR Limits:

Lenders typically set a maximum allowable TDSR, often around 44% with A lenders, and up to 48% with B lenders though this can vary. This limit represents the proportion of your income designated for servicing debts.

**Factors Impacting TDSR:**

> **Existing Debts:** The more debts you have, the higher your TDSR.
> **Income Level:** Higher income provides more flexibility within TDSR limits.

**TDSR and Borrowing Capacity:**

- **Optimal TDSR:** Aim for a TDSR below the lender's maximum to ensure financial flexibility.
- **Impact on Borrowing:** A lower TDSR enhances your eligibility for a mortgage.

**Holistic Financial Picture:**

TDSR is a crucial part of the comprehensive financial assessment that lenders undertake. Managing TDSR wisely ensures a balanced and sustainable approach to homeownership.

**Key Takeaways:**

- **Holistic Assessment:** TDSR considers all debts, providing a comprehensive view of your financial health.

- **Budget Planning:** Understanding TDSR helps you budget for both housing and non-housing debts responsibly.
- **Lender Criteria:** Explore lenders with TDSR thresholds aligning with your financial situation.

## Exceptional Lenders

It's important to highlight that certain standout lenders operate outside the confines of traditional GDS and TDS metrics. These exceptional lenders prioritize lending decisions based on the inherent strengths of both the property and the borrowers. Notably, such lenders exclusively reside in the realm of B-side financing.

# Secured versus unsecured debt

The influence of additional debts, whether secured or unsecured, plays a significant role in your mortgage application. When dealing with secured debts, such as a line of credit linked to a property, lenders typically consider only the interest-only monthly payment in their assessment. Conversely, for unsecured loans like **credit cards** or unsecured credit lines, they typically incorporate 3% of the used balance into the application evaluation. Understanding this distinction is crucial when managing your debt portfolio in the context of mortgage approval.

## Banks encourage secured borrowing

If you already own a house and your mortgage Broker has strategically secured a line of credit (HELOC) on that property, and you're considering using $40,000 from either your secured HELOC or an unsecured line, let's compare the two scenarios. Specifically, let's examine the implications of borrowing $40,000 from a secured line at 5%, involving an interest-only payment, against borrowing the same amount from an unsecured line at 3% of the balance.

Now, let's reassess the scenario of using $40,000 from a secured line of credit (HELOC) with a 5% interest rate (interest-only payment) compared to opting for an unsecured line of credit at 3% of the balance.

Secured Line of Credit (HELOC) at 5%:

- Annual Interest: $40,000 * 5% = $2,000
- Monthly Payment: $2,000 / 12 = $166.67

Unsecured Line of Credit at 3% of Balance:

- Monthly Payment: $40,000 * 3% = $1,200

The analysis indicates that utilizing the secured line of credit for the down payment is advantageous due to its lower monthly obligation. This choice minimizes the impact on the Total Debt Service (TDS) ratio in your mortgage application. It underscores the importance of strategic financial decisions aligned with your overall goals. The key word to remember is that banks incentivize and encourage secured lending, so lean towards it."

The lenders will use these numbers for calculations regardless of you actually making those payments or not. This is a risk calculation on the application.

To increase your borrowing capacity always use secured funds or liquidated funds like cash and savings.

## Thinking outside the Box

Before we dive into this I should
mention that I am a big fan of
thinking outside the box and
Thinking Different; One of the
reasons that makes me a big
fan of Steve Jobs is as well this
same strategy of thinking differently. I am also admiring
Codie Sanchez for her contrary thinking approach to
business building and I follow her on youtube. (I am not
promoting anyone and I am not paid for this. This is my
personal opinion). Back to the idea;

Buy more properties and continue to rent

Looking to buy a house but also want to live in your
rental? This scenario often arises with investors
who approach property purchases with a focus on
generating income and maximizing POSITIVE cash
flow. Investors may opt for properties in less
desirable neighborhoods or with lower home quality
to enhance their returns.

However, if you plan to live in your rental property,
there are considerations when it comes to

mortgage applications. Lenders will request a copy of the lease for your primary residence and factor in the monthly rent liability. This inclusion can impact your Total Debt Service (TDS) ratio.

In cases where you live with your parents, lenders may use an economical rent figure (which is lower than the regular rent) to factor into the application. Sometimes, depending on the specific circumstances of the file, lenders may provide exemptions and not factor in this rent, but it varies from case to case.

# How to qualify for more money?

The questions that make us all excited!

Meet **Adam and Jasmin,** a young couple with dreams of homeownership. Eager to step into the real estate game, they decided to explore their mortgage options. Using an online calculator, they discovered they could qualify for a mortgage of around $400,000. Excited but realizing it might limit their choices in the competitive housing market, they sought guidance.

However, when they approached their local bank, they were told that $400,000 was the maximum mortgage amount they could qualify for. Determined not to settle for less, they reached out to me, their mortgage  advisor. After a thorough assessment of their financial situation, I noticed a couple of opportunities to improve their mortgage eligibility. The couple had an outstanding OSAP (Ontario Student Assistance Program) loan with a relatively high monthly payment and a small remaining balance on a car loan.

Working closely with Adam and Jasmin, I devised a plan. We strategically lowered their OSAP monthly payment, creating more room in their budget. Additionally, we decided to pay off the remaining balance on the car loan, further reducing their monthly obligations. These adjustments had a positive domino effect, significantly improving their debt-to-income ratio. (Pic:New York Times)

As part of the strategy, I informed them that they could extend the repayment period of OSAP to 14.5 years, providing additional flexibility in managing their finances. With these changes implemented, Adam and Jasmin's financial profile underwent a transformation. Now, armed with a healthier financial picture, they found themselves eligible for a higher mortgage amount than initially calculated. This newfound financial flexibility opened doors to a broader range of properties, allowing them to explore homes that better aligned with their dreams. It's worth mentioning that knowing and caring to know about other things like OSAP and things that can impact my client is part of my care circle and that's what sets me apart. To my fellow brokers who are reading this book; if you get to care and go above and beyond you will be chosen as our client's broker for life. All for #**Broker_**

**For_Life**

The story of Adam and Jasmin highlights the importance of personalized mortgage advice and the potential impact of strategic financial planning.

By addressing specific elements of their financial landscape, we not only enhanced their eligibility but also empowered them to make more informed decisions on their homeownership journey.

## *Advice to Fellow Brokers: For those reading this, always strive to go above and beyond for your client*

**Advice to Fellow Brokers:** For those reading this, always strive to go above and beyond for your clients. Caring deeply and providing tailored solutions can establish you as their 'broker for life.'

## Credit Score and Report

It's not an over exaggeration if I say that in the eye of a bank your credit shows your character, Literally!

It's not uncommon to encounter the mindset of "My credit score is high, so don't ask me any questions!" However, understanding the reality behind credit scores is crucial. While a high credit score is undoubtedly positive, it's just one piece of the puzzle within a comprehensive credit report. **A**

# high credit score also means under utilized. Under utilized is as bad as over utilized.

Banks typically look for a credit history of at **least two years,** showcasing responsible use of **two major credit cards/Accounts and phone account**

**counts as credit accounts** with on-time payments. It's essential to keep credit utilization below 70%, meaning not exceeding 70% of the credit limit on a monthly basis. Additionally, the frequency of applying for new credit matters. Ideally, keeping the number of credit cards to a maximum of two is advisable.

For many A lenders, a credit score of 680 and above, as reported by Equifax, is preferred (we generally like to see a score of 700, as it can change slightly after we pull the scores internally from what consumers see on their end). ALLOW SOME WIGGLE ROOM. Some credit unions may work with lower credit scores, but as scores decrease, they might impose limitations on the loan-to-value ratio, often lending only up to 60% of the property's value. B lenders are even more flexible, considering applicants with scores as low as 500.

In essence, while a high credit score is an asset, the narrative within the credit report, including responsible credit card use and history, holds equal importance. Understanding these nuances is key to navigating the mortgage landscape successfully.

Having an excellence score but a blank report is equally as bad as having a bad credit report and score. **The Key in CREDIT is in responsible (on time pay back) and Reasonable *(40% of limit) use.**

# Responsible and Reasonable Use of credit is KEY.

## Checking your credit score and report regularly

This is a smart and proactive financial habit. Monitoring your credit allows you to stay informed about your financial health, detect any inaccuracies or unauthorized activities, and take steps to address them promptly. Here are some key reasons why checking your credit score and report is important. Think **of it as a health check-up for your finances. Staying on top of your credit helps you spot inaccuracies, prevent identity theft, and understand your financial standing:**

**Identity Theft Protection:** Regular monitoring helps you identify any suspicious or unauthorized activities that may indicate identity theft. If you notice unfamiliar accounts or transactions, you can take immediate action to address the issue.

**Accuracy of Information:** Mistakes can happen, and inaccuracies on your credit report may negatively impact your credit score. By reviewing your report regularly, you can catch and dispute any errors, ensuring that your credit information is correct.

**Credit Score Awareness:** Your credit score is a crucial factor in determining your creditworthiness. Regularly checking your score helps you understand where you stand financially and how lenders may perceive your creditworthiness.

**Financial Planning:** Monitoring your credit allows you to track your progress over time. If you're planning to make a significant financial move, such as applying for a mortgage or a new credit card, knowing your credit score in advance helps you make more informed decisions.

**Early Detection of Issues:** If there are negative changes to your credit report, such as late payments or accounts in collections, early detection allows you to address these issues promptly. Taking action quickly can minimize the impact on your credit score.

To check your credit score and report, you can use free services like Borrowell. However, please be cautious, as while Borrowell is a free service, they make money by encouraging people to sign up for credit cards. It's advisable to use their services solely for regularly checking your credit report.(I am not promoting Borrowell but they seem to be the only FREE service that gives you Equifax credit reports, all other Free services like Credit KARMA and others are retrieving Transunion) Banks mainly use Equifax. Stay vigilant and proactive to maintain a healthy credit profile. Note that while both Equifax and TransUnion are major credit bureaus, the majority of banks often work with Equifax.

Pulling your own credit report, often referred to as a "soft inquiry" or "soft pull," does not impact your credit score. This type of inquiry is considered a routine check that you initiate for personal reasons, and it's distinct from "hard inquiries" that occur when a lender checks your credit report in response to a credit application.

Given that checking your own credit report doesn't affect your score, you can do it as frequently as needed without worrying about negative repercussions. Regularly monitoring your credit report is a proactive and responsible financial practice, allowing you to stay informed about your credit status, detect any errors, and address potential issues promptly. It's a key aspect of maintaining good financial health.

Additionally, being vigilant about checking your credit report helps you identify any unauthorized or suspicious activity early on. This early detection can be crucial in preventing and addressing identity theft or fraudulent activities. By staying proactive in monitoring your credit, you empower yourself to maintain financial security and address any discrepancies promptly.

**Protect your credit as you would of your character**

**There I said it, I can be more bold and blunt than that. Your credit is indeed your character. Do you deliver on your promises; Your credit shows it all.**

**After all, your credit is your character indicator. The hardest thing in the five Cs of credit in my opinion to build is the first C which is Character. It takes time. Credit likewise it takes time.**

Safeguarding your credit is paramount, and how your credit is pulled can impact your score. Instead of individually approaching each banker or mortgage person and allowing multiple credit pulls, consider working with a mortgage broker. A broker can pull your credit once and leverage that information to shop around with various lenders on your behalf. This strategic approach minimizes the impact on your credit score while ensuring you find the best mortgage terms and rates. It's a win-win strategy for protecting your credit and securing favorable mortgage options. Additionally, you can take a proactive step by obtaining a copy of your Equifax credit report and sharing it with your advisor. This way, there's no need for them to pull a new report, further safeguarding your credit score.

## Down Payment: Setting the Foundation - Skin in the game!

 When it comes to purchasing a home, the down payment serves as the bedrock of your financial commitment. It's the initial investment you make towards homeownership, and understanding its significance is crucial.

1. Determining the Down Payment Amount

The down payment amount is typically expressed as a percentage of the total purchase price of the property. Traditionally, a 20% down payment has been considered standard practice, as it allows buyers to avoid Default Insurance ranges from 3-5% depending on the percentage of your D, and may secure more favorable mortgage terms. However, many lenders offer options for down payments as low as 3% (only in US) and 5% (in Canada) particularly for first-time homebuyers or those with excellent credit.

2. Importance of a Healthy Down Payment

A substantial down payment not only reduces the amount you need to borrow but also demonstrates financial stability to lenders. It signifies your commitment to the property and lowers the risk for the lender, potentially leading to better mortgage terms and lower interest rates.

## 3. Sources of Down Payment Funds

Down payment funds can come from various sources, including personal savings, investments, gifts from family members, or proceeds from the sale of existing assets. Some homebuyer assistance programs or employer-sponsored initiatives may also provide financial support for down payments.

## 4. Considerations for Different Types of Properties

The required down payment amount may vary based on factors such as the type of property you're purchasing. While a 20% down payment is often recommended for conventional mortgages on primary residences, higher down payments may be required for investment properties or vacation homes. sometimes up to 35% down or more.

## 5. Budgeting for Additional Costs

In addition to the down payment, homebuyers should budget for closing costs, which typically range from 2% to 5% of the purchase price. These costs cover expenses such as appraisal fees, title insurance, and legal fees, and should be factored into your overall home buying budget.

## 6. Flexibility and Creativity

In today's diverse mortgage landscape, there are numerous options for structuring down payments to suit individual circumstances. Whether you're exploring down payment assistance programs, leveraging retirement funds, or considering seller concessions, creativity and flexibility can open doors to homeownership.

## 7. Consultation and Guidance

Navigating the intricacies of down payments and mortgage options can be daunting, but you don't have to go it alone. Seeking guidance from a knowledgeable mortgage Broker can provide clarity and peace of mind as you embark on your home buying journey.

In essence, the down payment serves as the cornerstone of your investment in homeownership. By understanding its nuances and exploring your options, you can lay a solid foundation for your future in the real estate market.

## Zero Down Mortgages - Exploring the Magic

The magic of a zero down mortgage is a cash back mortgage which comes with a higher interest and the lender will give five percent cashback to the buyer at closing in order to use as Down payment figuratively and basically in plain simple terms the client ends up buying a property with Zero down. The side effect is that it will cost the client more on the interest side and is recommended if you have a really sweet deal on the buying side meaning the property you are buying is really worth it and is on fire sale price **which is rare but possible and investors with the right mindset find them everyday. They excel everyday and live an excellent everyday life. Be one and make your life a masterpiece. Your investment should be a masterpiece as well.**

**The cashback mortgages are no longer offered in the federally regulated banks due to the government ban.  Please do not mix this up with the regular cash back mortgages that after closing the bank gives you around $2000 more or less for getting a mortgage with them. That's a promotion.**

The allure of a zero down mortgage often revolves around a cash back mortgage option. This arrangement involves the lender providing a cashback incentive, typically around five percent of the purchase price, to the buyer at closing. This cash can then be used as a down payment, effectively allowing the buyer to acquire the property without putting any of their own money down.

However, this seemingly magical solution comes with a trade-off. Zero down mortgages usually come with slightly higher interest rates, which means that over the life of the loan, the buyer ends up paying more in interest. As such, this option is recommended only in specific scenarios. Rarely. The benefit of knowing this is that you will no longer be fooled by the fake advertisers and the people who put all those big signs in your face and you are puzzled as to what their magic might be! No one no longer can fool you again once you read this book entirely and rinse and repeat with us.

Zero down mortgages can be a viable option for some buyers, but they come with higher costs and risks. They require a keen eye for exceptional property deals and a thorough understanding of long-term financial implications. As always, thorough due diligence and consulting with a knowledgeable mortgage advisor are essential steps in navigating this option effectively

So next time when you drive by and see a sign saying Zero Down mortgages don't think they are magic workers and own the confidence that you read this book and now you know.

## Residential Income Property: Unlocking Passive Income Potential - The Game

Investing in residential income properties is like entering a strategic game with the potential for high rewards. These investments can provide steady income and build wealth over time. Let's dive into the essentials of this investment strategy.

### What is a Residential Income Property?

A residential income property is a real estate asset that generates rental income from tenants who occupy the property. These properties can range from single-family homes and condominiums to multi-unit properties up to 4 units - some lenders on exceptional basis consider a five-plex under residential lending. The Down payment for any type of rental property is 20%.

## Benefits of Investing in Residential Income Properties

1. Passive Income: Rental income from tenants provides a steady stream of passive income, which can supplement or replace earned income from other sources.
2. Asset Appreciation: Over time, residential properties often appreciate in value, allowing investors to build equity and potentially realize capital gains upon sale.
3. Tax Advantages: Investors may benefit from various tax deductions and incentives related to property ownership, such as

mortgage interest deductions, depreciation, and property tax deductions.
4. Diversification: Real estate investments offer diversification benefits, as they typically have low correlations with traditional financial assets like stocks and bonds.

Factors to Consider When Investing

1. Location: The location of the property plays a crucial role in its potential for rental income and appreciation. Factors such as proximity to amenities, job centers, schools, and transportation can impact demand from tenants.
2. Cash Flow Analysis: Conducting a thorough cash flow analysis is essential to determine the property's potential income and expenses. Consider factors such as rental market trends, vacancy rates, property management costs, and maintenance expenses. Email me at; hameed@hameedabdi.com for a Deal Analyzer Excel sheet. This deal analyzer is

the best tool ever the A-Team has built. We use it everyday for every deal.

3. Financing Options: Explore financing options tailored to investment properties, such as investment property loans or portfolio loans. Evaluate the terms, interest rates, and down payment requirements to optimize your financing strategy.

4. Property Management: Decide whether to manage the property yourself or hire a professional property management company. Property management entails responsibilities such as tenant screening, rent collection, property maintenance, and addressing tenant issues.

Risks and Challenges

1. **Vacancy Risk:** Periods of vacancy can impact cash flow and require investors to cover expenses out of pocket.

2. **Market Risk:** Real estate markets are subject to fluctuations in supply and demand, interest rates, and economic conditions,

which can affect property values and rental income.

3. **Regulatory Risk:** Changes in local regulations, zoning laws, or tenant protection laws can impact property operations and profitability.

**Long-Term Wealth Building**

Investing in residential income properties can be a cornerstone of a long-term wealth-building strategy. By acquiring and managing properties strategically, investors can generate consistent cash flow, build equity, and achieve financial independence over time.

In summary, residential income properties offer investors an opportunity to generate passive income, build equity, and diversify their investment portfolios. However, success in this asset class requires careful due diligence, market analysis, and a long-term investment mindset.

**Reminder;**

Lenders usually insist on borrowers having a personal stake in the investment, your "skin in the game," by requiring the down payment to be sourced from the borrower's own finances and their own equity from already owned properties.

This demonstrates the borrower's commitment and reduces the lender's risk.lenders generally prefer seeing that the down payment comes from the borrower's funds. This ensures the borrower's financial stability and ability to manage the mortgage responsibly. Financial aid programs, such as grants or loans, are typically aimed at assisting homebuyers, especially first-time buyers, and are not commonly available for real estate investors purchasing rental properties.

These programs are intended to help individuals or families achieve homeownership by covering the initial costs.

Investors looking to buy rental properties are generally expected to provide the down payment from their own resources, emphasizing the importance of having sufficient funds and showcasing the investor's dedication to the property.

Notes:

- Gifted down payments are not permitted on rental properties
- For when a gift down payment is accepted under owner occupied properties only a family member can gift you which includes; Parent, Grand parent, siblings, Spouse, Son or daughter

## Your Equity from your current home can fund your rental down payment.

All you have to do is have a Heloc in place on your existing property or ETO REFI it!

ETO means Equity Take out and REFI is Refinance. Doing an ETO REFI can give you significant cash to invest into rental properties.

Utilizing the equity from your current home through a Home Equity Line of Credit (HELOC) can be an effective way to fund the down payment for a rental property. With a HELOC in place, you can access the equity you've built up in your home by borrowing against it. HELOC has a limitation of up to 65% access to equity thus I always recommend ETO REFI and then I advise my clients to go and invest the money in easy to liquid stock options while waiting to buy RE (Real Estate) starting from GIC ( Guaranteed Investment Certificates) all the way to Mutual funds and stocks and the rest of it. Do not self invest. Get a professional to do it. If you need someone I have a good friend that I can introduce you to; email me at hameed@hameedabdi.com and I will be glad to introduce you;  Put Invest with your friend in the subject. You Might Also explore the option of buying a Whole Life insurance plan and leverage it to borrow against the value of your Policy in order to invest into real estate rental business. I do consider investing in the real estate rental market a business. To not get off the topic there are 3 things that top 1% investors invest in;

# 1. ONESELF; Me, Myself and I

# 2. Businesses

# 3. Real Estate/ASSETS and keep in mind when you invest in real estate rentals its a Business meaning you are one step up! So do take that equity out and invest it for better returns and build your empire.

This strategy allows you to leverage the value of your existing property to finance the purchase of an investment property without tapping into your savings or other sources of funds. However, it's important to carefully consider the risks and benefits of using a HELOC for this purpose, including potential changes in interest rates and repayment terms, before proceeding. Sometimes an ETO REFI Is better than HELOC Funding.

## Buy with a friend - Joint Venture

Speaking of friends; they are the most valuable assets in anything, especially in Real estate world. Relationships are the most important thing in life.

Joint venture partners buying a rental property with a friend. How does it work? Simple you have to both be on the purchase agreement. Mortgage application and eventually on the title all funds should be their own sources. and everything else is the same

Entering into a joint venture partnership with a friend to purchase a rental property involves several key steps to ensure a smooth and successful transaction. First, both parties must be listed on the purchase agreement, indicating their equal ownership of the property. Additionally, when applying for a mortgage, both partners will need to be included in the application process, providing their financial information and documentation to the lender.

Once the mortgage is approved and the property is acquired, both partners will be listed on the title deed as co-owners. It's crucial to ensure that all funds used for the down payment and closing costs come from each partner's own financial resources, as lenders typically require this to demonstrate each partner's commitment and financial stability.

Throughout the ownership of the rental property, both partners will share responsibilities and decisions related to property management, maintenance, and rental income. It's essential to establish clear communication and expectations from the outset to avoid potential conflicts or misunderstandings down the line.

Overall, while buying a rental property with a friend can offer advantages such as shared financial resources and responsibilities, it's essential to approach the partnership with careful planning, transparency, and a solid understanding of each party's roles and obligations.

# OPM Other People's Money

Sources of OPM

Traditional Bank Loans: Conventional mortgages or investment property loans from banks.

Private Lenders: Individuals or institutions that provide loans at negotiated terms.

Joint Venture Partners: Collaborating with other investors to pool resources and share risks.

Seller Financing: The property seller provides financing directly to the buyer, often with flexible terms.

Benefits and Risks of OPM

Increased Purchasing Power: Leveraging OPM allows for acquiring more or higher-value properties than using personal funds alone.

Risk Mitigation: Sharing financial responsibility reduces personal risk and enhances investment flexibility.

Careful Assessment Required: Evaluate all financing terms, potential returns, and exit strategies to mitigate the inherent risks of leveraging OPM.

Advanced OPM Strategies

Some investors might use more aggressive strategies, such as securing investments through retirement savings plans (like RRSPs) or even using high-interest unsecured debt. While these methods can provide quick capital, they require:

Solid Exit Strategies: Ensure you have a plan to refinance or liquidate assets to repay high-cost debt.

Value-Added Investments: Focus on properties where improvements can significantly increase value and cash flow.

Rental Income: Enhancing Mortgage Applications

Positive cash flow from rental properties can significantly improve your mortgage application by boosting your lending ratios. Here's how:

Impact on Lending Ratios

Supplemental Income: Lenders consider rental income as additional income, improving your debt-to-income (DTI) ratio.

Increased Loan Eligibility: With rental income, you can qualify for larger loans and higher loan-to-value (LTV) ratios, enhancing your purchasing power.

Income Diversification: Rental income diversifies your income sources, making you less reliant on traditional employment, which lenders view positively.

Sometimes Investors get others to invest their RRSP with them or they go even riskier and use unsecured debt or even credit card debt to secure sweet deals just to get in but they are smart enough to have an exit strategy like renovating the property and increasing the value plus the cash flow and refinance to get money out and pay off all those high cost debts. The key is for the deal to be really good; the win is in the buy.

Assessing borrowers' debt-to-income (DTI) ratios, which measure the proportion of monthly income allocated to debt payments. Including rental income in the DTI calculation can help lower the borrower's overall debt burden and improve their debt management capacity.

**Increased Loan Eligibility:** By including rental income in the mortgage application, **borrowers can qualify for larger loan amounts** and higher loan-to-value (LTV) ratios. Rental income supplements the borrower's qualifying income, allowing them to afford more expensive properties or finance a greater percentage of the property's purchase price. This expanded borrowing capacity enables borrowers to leverage their real estate investments effectively and pursue larger investment opportunities.

Portfolio Diversification: Lenders may view rental income positively as it diversifies the borrower's income sources and reduces dependence on traditional employment income. Rental properties offer investors a source of passive income that can withstand economic downturns and market fluctuations. By incorporating rental income into the mortgage application, borrowers demonstrate their ability to generate multiple streams of income and mitigate financial risk.

Proof of Rental Income: To include rental income in the mortgage application, borrowers must provide evidence of rental income stability and reliability. This typically involves submitting rental agreements, lease agreements, and rental income statements or receipts. Lenders may also require rental property cash flow analyses or appraisals to verify the property's income-generating potential.

In summary, rental income plays a pivotal role in mortgage applications, bolstering lending ratios and enhancing borrowers' financing options. By leveraging rental income effectively, investors can optimize their real estate investments and achieve their long-term financial objectives.

Tip: A Negative cash flowing property will only reduce the total income and be a liability instead of a help so it's important for an investor to always buy properties that have positive cash flow and get rid of the ones that are cash flow negative in order to be able to expand and grow.

## Investor-Friendly Lenders: Maximizing Rental Income Potential

Investor-friendly lenders play a pivotal role in supporting real estate investors by offering tailored financing solutions that leverage the income potential of rental properties. One key factor that sets these lenders apart is their ability to utilize rental income to offset mortgage expenses, thereby enhancing borrowing capacity and improving debt-to-income ratios. Here's how investor-friendly lenders leverage rental income to facilitate real estate investment excellence:

1. Rental Income Consideration: Unlike traditional lenders that may focus solely on the borrower's personal income and credit history, investor-friendly lenders take rental income into account when evaluating mortgage applications. They recognize the income-generating potential of rental properties and factor this revenue into the borrower's overall financial profile. By considering rental income, these lenders can increase the borrower's debt-servicing ability, allowing them to qualify for larger loan amounts or more favorable terms.

2. Debt-Service Coverage Ratio (DSCR): Investor-friendly lenders often use the debt-service coverage ratio (DSCR) to assess the viability of rental properties as income-generating assets. The DSCR measures the property's ability to generate sufficient rental income to cover its operating expenses and mortgage payments. Investor-friendly lenders can

evaluate the cash flow potential of rental properties and make informed lending decisions.

3. Rental Offset Programs: Many investor-friendly lenders offer rental offset programs that allow borrowers to use a portion of their rental income to offset mortgage expenses. Under these programs, lenders may credit a percentage of the property's rental income towards the borrower's qualifying income, effectively reducing their debt obligations. By incorporating rental income into the borrower's income calculations, these programs enable investors to qualify for larger loan amounts or more competitive interest rates, enhancing their purchasing power and investment potential.

4. Flexible Underwriting Guidelines: Investor-friendly lenders typically have more flexible underwriting guidelines compared to

traditional banks, allowing them to accommodate a broader range of borrower profiles and property types. These lenders understand the nuances of real estate investing and can tailor financing solutions to meet the unique needs and objectives of investors. Whether financing single-family homes, multi-unit properties, or commercial real estate, investor-friendly lenders can structure loans that align with the borrower's investment strategy and property portfolio.

In summary, investor-friendly lenders play a critical role in maximizing the income potential of rental properties and facilitating real estate investment success. By considering rental income, leveraging rental offset programs, and employing flexible underwriting guidelines, these lenders empower investors to unlock the full value of their rental properties and achieve their investment goals.

Pro Tip: **Avoid properties** with **negative cash flow,** as they can become liabilities and hinder your financial growth. Focus on acquiring and maintaining properties that generate positive cash flow to support sustainable investment expansion Typically lenders include from 50% to 80% of the rental income into the application but there are lenders who include 100% of the rental income to qualify you for a loan. They are just rare.

# The only empire builder in Real Estate or any business is POSITIVE CASHFLOW!

**Rental income from Basement unit**

The only time you can use rental income from a basement unit is if the unit is legal. Lenders do not include rental income from secondary units if they are not legal units.

Legal units just cost a bit more but they are worth it. House hack and turn your

**basement into a rental unit.** You are sitting on gold right now.  You will thank me later.

## The Key Player; The Broker The RAINMAKER

A mortgage broker is a licensed financial professional who acts as GUIDE an intermediary between borrowers and lenders. They help individuals and  businesses secure the best mortgage terms (terms are more important than rates)  and rates for purchasing or refinancing real estate. Here's a closer look at the role and benefits of working with a mortgage broker:

**Role of a Mortgage Broker**

Assessment and Consultation:

- Initial Consultation: Mortgage brokers start by **assessing** the financial situation and needs of the borrower. This includes reviewing credit scores, income, **assets**, and debts.
- Mortgage Pre-Approval: They help borrowers get pre-approved for a mortgage, which provides an estimate of how much they can borrow.

Market Research:

- Access to **Multiple Lenders**: Brokers have access to a wide network of lenders, including banks, credit unions, and private lenders. This enables them to compare various mortgage products and find the best fit for the borrower.
- Rate Comparison: They compare interest rates and terms from different lenders to secure the **most favorable deal.**

Application Process:

- Documentation: Brokers assist in gathering and organizing all necessary documentation, such as tax returns, bank statements, and employment verification.
- Submission: They submit the mortgage application to the chosen lender on behalf of the borrower.

Negotiation and Advice:

- Negotiating Terms: Mortgage brokers negotiate with lenders to obtain the best terms and rates.
- Expert Advice: They provide expert advice on the various mortgage products available, explaining the pros and cons of each option.

Closing the Deal:

- Coordination: Brokers coordinate with all parties involved in the transaction, including real estate agents,

appraisers, and lawyers, to ensure a smooth closing process.
- Finalization: They help finalize the mortgage deal, ensuring all paperwork is completed correctly and on time.

**Benefits of Using a Mortgage Broker**

Wide Range of Options:

- Access to Multiple Lenders: Unlike a single bank or lender, brokers have access to a broad range of mortgage products from various institutions.
- Tailored Solutions: They can find mortgage options that are tailored to the specific needs and financial situations of different borrowers.

# Convenience:

- Time-Saving: Brokers handle the legwork of shopping around for the best mortgage rates

and terms, saving borrowers significant time and effort.
- Streamlined Process: They simplify the mortgage application process, helping borrowers navigate through complex requirements and paperwork.

## Expertise:

- Market Knowledge: Mortgage brokers have in-depth knowledge of the mortgage market and stay updated on the latest trends and changes.
- Professional Guidance: They provide professional guidance and advice, helping borrowers make informed decisions.

## Cost-Effective:

- Competitive Rates: By negotiating with lenders, brokers can often secure more competitive interest rates and better terms than borrowers might find on their own.

- Fee Transparency: They provide clear information about fees and costs associated with different mortgage options.

Conclusion

A mortgage broker plays a crucial role in the home buying and refinancing process, offering expertise, convenience, and access to a wide range of mortgage products. By working with a mortgage broker, borrowers can save time, money, and stress, ensuring they find the best mortgage solution for their needs.

# Financing with the Big Picture in Mind

Strategic Planning for Real Estate Investors

When working with real estate investors, it's essential to adopt a forward-thinking approach. This means not only focusing on the immediate financing needs but also considering future moves and long-term goals. Here's how strategic planning plays a crucial role in real estate investment success:

## 1. Understanding the Investor's Vision

### Long-Term Goals

Portfolio Growth: Identify the investor's aspirations for expanding their property portfolio. Determine the number and types of properties they aim to acquire over a specified period.

Financial Independence: Clarify how the investor envisions their passive income streams contributing to financial freedom or retirement plans.

### Risk Tolerance

Market Volatility: Assess the investor's comfort level with market fluctuations and economic cycles.

Investment Horizon: Determine the investor's timeline for holding properties, whether short-term flipping or long-term buy-and-hold strategies.

## 2. Tailoring Financing Solutions

Customized Loan Products

Flexible Mortgage Options: Offer mortgage products that accommodate the investor's specific needs, such as interest-only loans, adjustable-rate mortgages, or portfolio loans.

Future Refinancing: Plan for potential refinancing options that can free up equity for future investments.

Leveraging Equity

Home Equity Line of Credit (HELOC): Utilize the equity from existing properties to fund down payments for new acquisitions.

Cash-Out Refinancing: Refinance existing mortgages to extract cash for reinvestment while potentially securing better terms.

3. Planning for Future Acquisitions

Pre-Approval for Multiple Properties

Streamlined Approvals: Ensure that investors are pre-approved for additional properties, facilitating quicker acquisitions as opportunities arise.

Portfolio Loans: Consider portfolio loans that allow investors to finance multiple properties under a single loan agreement.

Building Relationships with Lenders

Preferred Investor Status: Cultivate strong relationships with investor-friendly lenders who understand and cater to the unique needs of real estate investors.

Negotiating Power: Use these relationships to negotiate favorable terms and conditions, leveraging the investor's track record and portfolio size.

## 4. Considering Market Trends and Economic Indicators

Market Analysis

Location Insights: Stay informed about emerging markets, property appreciation trends, and rental demand in different areas.

Economic Factors: Monitor interest rates, inflation rates, and economic policies that could impact real estate investments.

Future-Proofing Investments

Property Diversification: Encourage investors to diversify their portfolio across various property types and locations to mitigate risks.

Sustainable Practices: Consider the benefits of energy-efficient and sustainable properties, which can attract quality tenants and reduce operating costs.

## 5. Legal and Tax Considerations

### Structuring Investments

Legal Entities: Advise on the best legal structures for holding properties, such as LLCs or partnerships, to protect assets and optimize tax benefits.

Tax Planning: Work with tax professionals to develop strategies that minimize tax liabilities, including deductions for depreciation, mortgage interest, and property management expenses.

### Regulatory Compliance

Local Laws: Stay updated on local regulations affecting rental properties, zoning laws, and tenant rights.

Federal Changes: Be aware of federal tax law changes and their implications for real estate investments.

In summary, When financing real estate investments, it's vital to look beyond immediate needs and consider the broader picture. By understanding the investor's long-term goals, tailoring financing solutions, planning for future acquisitions, staying informed about market trends, and considering legal and tax implications, mortgage brokers can provide invaluable support. This strategic approach ensures that every move made today aligns with the investor's future success and financial independence.

## Your Reputation as a Borrower is Everything

In the world of real estate investing, your reputation as a borrower holds immense significance. It can influence your ability to secure favorable loan terms, expand your portfolio, and build lasting relationships with lenders and other financial professionals. Here's why maintaining a stellar reputation is crucial and how you can achieve it:

Why Your Borrower Reputation Matters

1. Access to Better Financing Options

Preferred Rates: Lenders offer better interest rates to borrowers with a proven track record of reliability and financial responsibility.

Flexible Terms: A strong reputation can lead to more flexible loan terms, including higher loan-to-value ratios and longer repayment periods.

2. Faster Approvals

Streamlined Process: Lenders are more likely to expedite loan approvals for borrowers they trust, reducing the time it takes to close deals.

Pre-Approval Advantage: Trusted borrowers often receive pre-approvals for multiple properties, allowing them to act quickly on new opportunities.

## 3. Increased Negotiating Power

Better Deals: A good reputation enhances your negotiating power, enabling you to secure more favorable terms and conditions.

Access to Exclusive Offers: Lenders may offer exclusive deals and programs to their most reliable borrowers.

Building and Maintaining a Strong Borrower Reputation

## 1. Timely Payments

Consistent On-Time Payments: Always make your mortgage and other debt payments on time. Late payments can significantly damage your credit score and lender trust.

Automated Payments: Consider setting up automated payments to ensure you never miss a due date.

## 2. Responsible Credit Management

Credit Utilization: Keep your credit utilization below 70%, meaning you shouldn't exceed 70% of your available credit limit.

Avoiding Excessive Credit Applications: Frequent applications for new credit can be a red flag. Limit your credit inquiries to essential needs.

## 3. Clear Communication

Transparency with Lenders: Keep open lines of communication with your lenders. If you foresee any issues with your payments, inform them proactively.

Regular Updates: Provide lenders with regular updates on your financial status and any significant changes that may impact your ability to repay loans.

4. Proper Documentation

Organized Records: Maintain organized and accurate financial records. This includes tax returns, income statements, and documentation of your assets and liabilities.

Full Disclosure: When applying for loans, provide complete and truthful information. Misrepresentation can severely damage your reputation.

5. Professional Relationships

Build Relationships: Cultivate strong relationships with mortgage brokers, real estate agents, and other financial professionals.

Networking: Attend industry events and engage with professionals to build a network that can vouch for your reliability and integrity.

Handling Challenges Effectively

## 1. Managing Financial Difficulties

Proactive Measures: If you encounter financial difficulties, take proactive measures to address them, such as restructuring your debt or negotiating new terms with your lender.

Seeking Assistance: Don't hesitate to seek assistance from financial advisors or credit counselors to manage your finances effectively.

## 2. Learning from Mistakes

Acknowledge Mistakes: If you've made financial mistakes in the past, acknowledge them and take steps to correct them.

Rebuilding Credit: Focus on rebuilding your credit by making consistent, on-time payments and reducing your overall debt load.

Your reputation as a borrower is a critical asset in the realm of real estate investment. By making timely payments, managing your credit responsibly, communicating clearly, maintaining proper documentation, and building professional relationships, you can establish and maintain a strong reputation. This reputation will open doors to better financing options, faster approvals, and greater negotiating power, ultimately contributing to your long-term success as a real estate investor.

# Appraisals and Borrowing Surprises: What You Need to Know

When you're in the process of purchasing or refinancing a property, appraisals play a crucial role in determining how much you can borrow. Understanding the appraisal process and being prepared for potential surprises can help you navigate this critical step with confidence.

## The Importance of Appraisals

An appraisal is an unbiased professional assessment of a property's value. Lenders use appraisals to ensure that the amount they are lending is in line with the property's market value. Here's why appraisals are essential:

- Loan Approval: The appraisal helps lenders decide whether to approve your loan and how much to lend.

- Risk Management: It mitigates the lender's risk by confirming that the property's value justifies the loan amount.
- Fair Market Value: Ensures that you're not overpaying for the property.

The Appraisal Process

## 1. Order and Schedule

- The lender orders the appraisal after you have signed the purchase agreement or initiated a refinance.
- An appraiser is then assigned to visit the property and conduct an evaluation.

## 2. Property Inspection

- The appraiser conducts a thorough inspection of the property, examining its condition, features, and any improvements.
- They also assess the property's location, comparing it with similar properties in the area (comps).

## 3. Research and Report

- The appraiser researches comparable property sales and market conditions.
- A detailed report is compiled, including the appraiser's opinion of the property's market value.

## Potential Borrowing Surprises

While the appraisal process is straightforward, several surprises can impact your borrowing experience:

## 1. Low Appraisal Value

- Impact: If the appraisal comes in lower than the purchase price, the lender may not approve the full loan amount.
- Solutions: You can renegotiate the purchase price, increase your down payment to cover the difference, or request a review of the appraisal.

## 2. Condition Issues

- Impact: The appraiser may note significant repairs or issues that affect the property's value.
- Solutions: Addressing these issues before the appraisal or negotiating with the seller to fix them can help mitigate this surprise.

## 3. Market Fluctuations

- Impact: Sudden changes in the real estate market can affect comparable sales and, consequently, the appraisal value.
- Solutions: Stay informed about market trends and work closely with your real estate agent and lender to set realistic expectations.

Preparing for the Appraisal

## 1. Understand the Process

- Educate yourself about how appraisals work and what factors influence property value.

## 2. Be Present

- While not always necessary, being present during the appraisal can help answer any questions the appraiser may have.

## 3. Document Improvements

- Provide the appraiser with a list of any recent upgrades or improvements to the property, including receipts and permits.

## 4. Maintain the Property

- Ensure the property is clean and well-maintained before the appraisal to make a good impression.

Handling Surprises

1. Stay Calm

- Unexpected appraisal results can be stressful, but staying calm and assessing your options is crucial.

2. Communicate

- Open lines of communication with your lender, real estate agent, and the appraiser can help address any concerns promptly.

3. Seek a Second Opinion

- If you believe the appraisal is significantly off, you can request a second appraisal or a review from another appraiser.

Appraisals are a vital part of the mortgage process, providing a reality check on property values and ensuring that both lenders and buyers make informed decisions. By understanding the appraisal process, preparing thoroughly, and being ready to address any surprises, you can smooth the path to securing your mortgage and achieving your real estate goals.

In this chapter we discussed the players of the MORTGAGE GAME. Stay with us in the next chapter where we can play with the plays and get creative with the rules and find the ways to win. How we win is what we are going to learn. We will discover the most important aspect of playing the Mortgage Game and playing it right.

# Chapter 2; Creativity and Rules

My Favorite Chapter, What is the most important ingredient to win in the Mortgage Game is **not to be scared**. Don't fear. **The only thing you need to fear is fear itself.(FDR)** Play by the rules and be creative and don't be scared. End of story, However we are just beginning the chapter. ALSO play by the rules; You can't widen the gate to make sure you shoot the Goal. This is a Mind and Mortgage Game. Everyday on my Newsletter "Hameed Daily" I discuss Mindset and Mortgage why I discuss mindset first. It is because Mindset is everything. It's the foundation of excellence in the Mortgage Game. Moving on.

Game on, understand the rules and the players is just a baby step, learning to play with them and utilize them to our advantage is what masters do and you will be a master once you study practice and teach this chapter, not just learn; study practice and teach as Jim Rohn said; always be studying, practicing and teaching. Let's do it. Or as NIKE put it JUST DO IT!

# How to Get Creative in the Mortgage Game in Canada: Strategies for Investors

Investing in real estate in Canada can be a profitable venture, but it requires a strategic approach to maximize your borrowing potential while adhering to regulations. Here are several creative strategies for investors looking to succeed in the Canadian mortgage market:

## 1. Leverage Existing Equity

Home Equity Line of Credit (HELOC): If you already own property, a HELOC allows you to tap into your existing equity to finance the down payment for new investments. This can be a powerful tool for expanding your real estate portfolio without needing liquid cash.

## 2. Explore Different Financing Options

Multi-Unit Residential Mortgages: Many lenders offer favorable terms for properties with multiple units (up to four units under residential lending). This can provide higher rental income streams and improve your debt service coverage ratio (DSCR).

Commercial Mortgages: For larger properties (five units or more), consider commercial mortgages. While they typically require higher down payments and have different qualifying criteria, they can offer more flexibility and larger loan amounts.

3. Joint Ventures and Partnerships

Joint Ventures: Partnering with other investors can help pool resources for down payments and share risks. Ensure all partners are on the purchase agreement, mortgage application, and title. Clearly define roles, responsibilities, and exit strategies in a joint venture agreement.

4. Maximize Rental Income

Secondary Suites and Multi-Unit Properties: Adding secondary suites or investing in multi-unit properties can significantly increase your rental income. Ensure compliance with local zoning laws and building codes.

Short-Term Rentals: Consider using platforms like Airbnb for properties in high-demand areas. Short-term rentals can generate higher income compared to long-term leases, but make sure to comply with local regulations.

5. Improve Your Financial Profile

Debt Consolidation: Pay off high-interest debts or consolidate them to improve your debt-to-income (DTI) ratio, making you more attractive to lenders.

Credit Improvement: Maintain a high credit score by paying bills on time, reducing credit card balances, and avoiding new debt. A higher score can qualify you for better mortgage rates.

6. Use Gift Funds

Gift Letters: If you receive financial help from family or friends for your down payment, provide a gift letter to the lender. This letter should state that the money is a gift and not a loan that needs to be repaid.

7. Investigate Down Payment Assistance Programs

Local and Provincial Programs: While most assistance programs are aimed at first-time homebuyers, some regions offer incentives for rental properties or multi-unit dwellings. Research what is available in your area and ensure you meet the eligibility requirements.

8. Buy and Renovate

Purchase Plus Improvements Program: This program allows investors to include renovation costs in their mortgage. This can be particularly beneficial if you're buying a property that needs upgrades to attract higher rental income.

## 9. Shop Around

Mortgage Brokers: Work with a mortgage broker who specializes in investment properties. They can shop around for the best mortgage deals on your behalf and find terms that suit your investment strategy.

## 10. Stay Informed and Compliant

Regulatory Knowledge: Stay up-to-date on mortgage lending regulations, tax laws, and market conditions in Canada. This knowledge will help you make informed decisions and avoid potential pitfalls.

You just studied the 10 excellence strategies to be the greatest investor of all time.

Professional Advice: Regularly consult with financial advisors, real estate agents, and mortgage

Brokers who have experience with investment properties to ensure your strategies are sound and compliant with current laws and regulations.

## Seller Financing (Vendor Take-Back) and RRSP Loans: Creative Financing Strategies for Investors in Canada

In the realm of real estate investment, utilizing creative financing strategies can provide investors with unique advantages. Two such strategies are Vendor Take-Back (Seller Financing) mortgages and RRSP loans. Both options can offer flexibility and potential cost savings, enabling investors to navigate the Canadian real estate market more effectively.

### Vendor Take-Back (Seller Financing) Mortgages

### What is a Seller Financing Mortgage?

A Vendor Take-Back (Seller Financing) mortgage is a type of financing where the seller of a property agrees to lend a portion of the purchase price to the buyer. This creates a mortgage that the buyer pays back directly to the seller, often at terms that can be more favorable than those offered by traditional lenders.

How Seller Financing Mortgages Work:

- Negotiation: The buyer and seller negotiate the terms of the Seller Financing mortgage, including the interest rate, repayment schedule, and any other conditions.
- Legal Documentation: The agreement is documented in the purchase and sale agreement and formalized through legal contracts.
- Repayment: The buyer makes regular mortgage payments directly to the seller, as agreed upon.

Advantages of Seller Financing Mortgages:

- Flexibility: Seller Financing mortgages can offer more flexible terms than traditional mortgages, including lower interest rates or extended repayment periods.
- Easier Qualification: Buyers who might not meet the strict criteria of conventional lenders can still secure financing.
- Win-Win Situation: Sellers can sell their property more quickly and potentially earn interest income, while buyers gain access to financing they might not otherwise obtain.

Considerations:

- Risk: Sellers take on the risk of the buyer defaulting on the mortgage.
- Due Diligence: Both parties should conduct thorough due diligence and consult legal and financial advisors to ensure the agreement is fair and legally sound.

RRSP Loans

What is an RRSP Loan?

An RRSP (Registered Retirement Savings Plan) loan involves borrowing money from your RRSP to invest in real estate. In Canada, the Home Buyers' Plan (HBP) allows first-time homebuyers to withdraw up to $35,000 from their RRSPs tax-free to purchase or build a home.

How RRSP Loans Work:

- Eligibility: Verify that you are eligible for the HBP, which requires that you be a first-time homebuyer or meet certain criteria.
- Withdrawal: Withdraw the desired amount from your RRSP, up to the HBP limit.
- Repayment: Repay the withdrawn amount to your RRSP over a period of up to 15 years. Payments must start in the second year following the year of withdrawal.

Advantages of RRSP Loans:

- Tax-Free Withdrawal: Funds withdrawn under the HBP are not subject to immediate taxation.
- Access to Funds: Provides access to funds for a down payment without incurring early withdrawal penalties.
- Investment Growth: The withdrawn funds can be used to invest in real estate, potentially yielding higher returns.

Considerations:

- Repayment Obligation: The withdrawn amount must be repaid to the RRSP according to the HBP schedule. Failure to do so results in the amount being included in taxable income.
- Opportunity Cost: Withdrawn funds no longer grow tax-free within the RRSP, potentially affecting long-term retirement savings.

Combining Seller Financing and RRSP Loans

Strategic Use:

Investors can combine Seller Financing mortgages and RRSP loans to maximize their financing options. For example, an investor could use RRSP funds for a portion of the down payment while negotiating a Seller Financing mortgage for additional financing. This strategy can reduce the amount borrowed from traditional lenders and improve cash flow.

Investing in real estate in Canada requires creativity and strategic planning to maximize your borrowing potential and achieve your financial goals. By leveraging existing equity, exploring different financing options, maximizing rental income, and staying informed about regulatory changes, you can navigate the mortgage landscape effectively. Always seek professional advice to ensure your investment strategies align with your long-term objectives and comply with Canadian regulations.

Seller Financing mortgages and RRSP loans offer creative and flexible financing options for real estate investors in Canada. By understanding and leveraging these strategies, investors can secure favorable terms, reduce borrowing costs, and enhance their investment potential. Always seek advice from financial and legal professionals to ensure these strategies align with your overall investment goals and comply with Canadian regulations.

## A seller may agree to a Vendor Take-Back (Seller Financing) mortgage for several reasons, including:

1. Faster Sale: Offering financing through a Seller Financing mortgage can attract more potential buyers and speed up the sale process. This is especially beneficial in a slow market where finding qualified buyers may be challenging.

2. Higher Sale Price: Sellers can often negotiate a higher sale price when offering financing through a Seller Financing mortgage. Buyers may be willing to pay more for the property to secure favorable financing terms.

3. Interest Income: By financing a portion of the sale price, sellers can earn interest income on the mortgage payments made by the buyer. This provides an additional source of revenue for the seller.

4. Flexible Terms: Sellers have the flexibility to negotiate the terms of the Seller Financing mortgage, including the interest rate, repayment schedule, and any other conditions. This allows sellers to tailor the financing arrangement to their specific needs and preferences.

5. Asset Security: If the buyer defaults on the Seller Financing mortgage, the seller can foreclose on the property and regain ownership. This provides a level of security for the seller in case of default.

6. Attracting Buyers with Limited Financing Options: Offering financing through a Seller Financing mortgage can attract buyers who may not qualify for traditional bank financing due to credit issues, insufficient down payment, or other reasons.

Overall, a Seller Financing mortgage can be a win-win solution for both sellers and buyers, providing sellers with a competitive advantage in the market and allowing buyers to purchase a property with favorable financing terms.

Deferring taxes under Vendor Take-Back (Seller Financing) financing involves a seller providing financing to the buyer of a property, allowing the buyer to defer paying a portion of the purchase price upfront. This arrangement can have tax implications for both the seller and the buyer:

For the Seller:

1. Capital Gains Tax Deferral: By spreading out the receipt of the sale proceeds over time through Seller Financing financing, the seller may be able to defer paying capital gains tax on the full amount of the sale until the payments are received. This can be advantageous for sellers looking to minimize their immediate tax liability.
2. Interest Income: The seller earns interest income on the financing provided to the buyer, which is taxable in the year it is received. However, because the payments are spread out over time, the seller may have the opportunity to manage their taxable income more effectively by receiving payments in different tax years.

For the Buyer:

1. Immediate Tax Implications: The buyer may still be responsible for paying taxes on any capital gains realized from the purchase of the property, even if they are deferring a portion of the purchase price through Seller Financing financing. However, spreading out the payments over time may allow the buyer to manage their cash flow and tax obligations more effectively.
2. Interest Expense Deduction: The interest paid to the seller as part of the Seller Financing financing arrangement may be deductible for tax purposes, depending on the buyer's specific circumstances and the tax laws in their jurisdiction. This can help offset the cost of financing and reduce the buyer's overall tax liability.

It's essential for both parties involved in a Seller Financing financing arrangement to consult with tax professionals or financial advisors to fully understand the tax implications and benefits of deferring taxes in this manner. Additionally, the terms of the Seller Financing agreement should be carefully negotiated and documented to ensure compliance with tax laws and regulations.

## Cautionary Considerations

Caution is indeed warranted when considering seller financing, and thorough review of the terms and conditions is essential before entering into any agreement. Here are some key points to consider and potential risks associated with Seller Financing financing:

Legal and Financial Risks: Seller Financing financing involves complex legal and financial arrangements that require careful consideration. It's crucial to seek advice from legal and financial professionals who specialize in real estate transactions to ensure that you fully understand the terms of the agreement and the potential risks involved.

Interest Rates and Terms: The interest rates and repayment terms of Seller Financing financing may differ from traditional mortgage loans. Buyers should carefully review these terms to ensure they are competitive and favorable compared to other financing options available to them.

Default and Foreclosure: In the event of default on Seller Financing financing, the seller may have the right to foreclose on the property and take legal action to recover any outstanding debts. Buyers should be aware of the consequences of default and foreclosure under Seller Financing financing arrangements.

Prepayment Penalties: Some Seller Financing agreements may include prepayment penalties if the buyer wishes to pay off the loan early. Buyers should review these provisions carefully and consider the potential impact on their financial flexibility and ability to refinance in the future.

Title and Ownership: Seller Financing financing arrangements may involve complex legal issues related to title and ownership of the property. Buyers should conduct thorough due diligence to ensure that the seller has clear title to the property and that there are no outstanding liens or encumbrances that could affect ownership rights.

Negotiation and Documentation: It's essential to negotiate and document the terms of the Seller Financing agreement carefully to protect the interests of both parties. This may include specifying the repayment schedule, interest rates, and any other conditions or contingencies that need to be addressed.

Overall, while Seller Financing financing can offer benefits such as flexibility in financing and tax deferral, it's essential to approach these arrangements with caution and ensure that you fully understand the risks and obligations involved. Seeking professional advice and conducting thorough due diligence can help mitigate potential risks and ensure a successful transaction.

## How to buy a property with Zero(Nothing-No Money) Down?

Buying a property with zero down payment is possible, but it typically involves specific strategies and considerations. Here are some options to explore:

- Government Programs: In some countries, government programs offer assistance to first-time homebuyers, including down payment assistance grants or loans. These programs may provide funds to cover some or all of the down payment required to purchase a home.

- Gift Funds: Buyers may receive gift funds from family members or other sources to use toward the down payment. Lenders typically require a gift letter confirming that the funds are a gift and not a loan that needs to be repaid.

- Seller Financing: In a seller financing arrangement, the seller agrees to finance part or all of the purchase price of the property. This can include a Vendor Take-Back (Seller Financing) mortgage or lease-to-own agreement, where the buyer pays the seller directly over time.

- Down Payment Assistance Programs: Some organizations or nonprofits offer down payment assistance programs to help homebuyers cover the upfront costs of purchasing a home. These programs may provide grants, loans, or other forms of assistance to eligible buyers.

- **Rent-to-Own:** In a rent-to-own arrangement, the buyer rents the property with the option to purchase it at a later date. A portion of the rent payments may be credited toward the down payment or purchase price of the home.

### Pros of Rent-to-Own

1. **Build Equity Over Time**: Part of your rent payments typically goes toward the purchase price, allowing you to build equity while renting.
2. **Lock in Purchase Price**: The purchase price is often agreed upon at the start of the lease, which can be advantageous if property values rise over the rental period.

3. **Credit Improvement**: Rent-to-own can be a good option for buyers who need time to improve their credit score. Consistent rent payments can help demonstrate financial responsibility.

4. **Test Living in the Home**: You get to live in the property and neighborhood before making a long-term commitment, ensuring it meets your needs and preferences.

5. **Potential Savings**: If property values increase significantly, locking in a purchase price early can save money compared to buying outright later.

### Cons of Rent-to-Own

1. **Non-Refundable Fees**: Option fees and rent premiums paid for the option to purchase are

typically non-refundable if you decide not to buy the property.

2. **Higher Rent Payments**: Rent payments are often higher than the market rate to cover the option to purchase and any rent credits.

3. **Uncertain Financing**: Securing a mortgage at the end of the rental period is not guaranteed. If you can't get financing, you might lose the option fee and any rent credits accumulated.

4. **Property Condition Risks**: The condition of the property might deteriorate, and you could be responsible for maintenance and repairs depending on the terms of the agreement.

5. **Market Fluctuations**: If the market value of the property decreases, you might end up paying more than the current market price.

6. **Contract Complexity**: Rent-to-own agreements can be complex and require careful

legal review to ensure fair terms and protect your interests.

- Piggyback Loans: A piggyback loan involves taking out two mortgages simultaneously, with one covering the down payment and the other covering the remaining purchase price. This can help buyers avoid private mortgage insurance (PMI) and secure financing with zero down. You just need to be able to afford carrying the mortgages. A sweet deal will allow that.

Creative Financing: Buyers can explore creative financing options, such as borrowing against other assets, using retirement funds, or leveraging equity from existing properties to cover the down payment.

It's essential to carefully consider the risks and benefits of each option and consult with a financial advisor or mortgage professional to determine the best approach for your individual circumstances. Additionally, buyers should be aware of potential drawbacks, such as higher interest rates, stricter eligibility requirements, and long-term financial implications, when pursuing zero down payment options.

## A Crucial Point

Keep in mind, Even if you secure a property with zero down payment, there are still closing costs associated with the purchase that you'll need to cover. These costs typically range from 3% to 6% sometimes more of the purchase price and can include expenses such as:

1. Title Insurance: Protects against defects in the property title.

2. Appraisal Fees: Covers the cost of assessing the property's value.
3. Home Inspection: Ensures the property is in good condition and identifies any issues.
4. Legal Fees: Covers the cost of legal services, including document preparation and review.
5. Property Taxes: Prepaid taxes for the portion of the year you'll own the property.
6. Recording Fees: Fees paid to record the property sale with the local government.
7. Loan Origination Fees: Charged by the lender for processing the loan application.
8. Escrow Fees: Covers the cost of managing funds and documents during the closing process.

It's essential for buyers to budget for these closing costs in addition to any down payment requirements. While securing a property with zero down payment can help reduce upfront expenses, buyers should be prepared to cover these additional costs to complete the purchase transaction. Working with a knowledgeable real estate agent or financial advisor can help buyers understand and plan for these expenses effectively.

## Joint ventures (JVs) in real estate investing

It involves pooling resources, expertise, and capital with one or more partners to undertake a property investment project. Here's how to navigate joint ventures effectively: JV parties may /may not be on the title & still have secured interest in the properties.

1. Identify Compatible Partners: Look for partners who share your investment goals, risk tolerance, and work ethic. Compatibility is crucial for a successful joint venture.
2. Define Roles and Responsibilities: Clearly outline each partner's roles and responsibilities in the joint venture agreement. This includes tasks such as property acquisition, financing, property management, and decision-making processes.
1. Establish Trust and Communication: Foster open communication and trust among partners. Regular meetings and updates ensure everyone is aligned with project objectives and decisions.
2. Agree on Investment Criteria: Define investment criteria, including property type,

location, budget, expected returns, and exit strategy. Consensus on these factors minimizes conflicts and ensures everyone is on the same page.

3. Create a Joint Venture Agreement: Draft a comprehensive joint venture agreement outlining terms, responsibilities, profit-sharing arrangements, dispute resolution mechanisms, and exit strategies. Consult legal and financial professionals to ensure the agreement is legally binding and protects all parties' interests.

4. Conduct Due Diligence: Thoroughly research potential investment opportunities, including property assessments, market analysis, financial projections, and legal considerations. Due diligence helps mitigate risks and ensures informed investment decisions.

5. Secure Financing: Determine the financing structure for the joint venture, including capital contributions from each partner and external financing options. Evaluate various financing sources, such as traditional mortgages, private lenders, or self-directed retirement accounts.

6. Execute the Investment Plan: Once the joint venture agreement is in place and financing secured, proceed with property acquisition, renovation (if necessary), and property management. Regular monitoring and reporting keep partners informed of project progress.

7. Monitor Performance and Adjust as Needed: Track the investment's performance against established goals and benchmarks. If necessary, make adjustments to the investment strategy, property management approach, or exit timeline to optimize returns and mitigate risks.

8. Communicate and Evaluate: Maintain ongoing communication with joint venture partners and conduct periodic evaluations of the investment's performance. Assessing outcomes against initial projections helps identify areas for improvement and informs future investment decisions.

By following these steps and collaborating effectively with joint venture partners, real estate investors can leverage collective expertise and resources to pursue profitable investment opportunities while minimizing risks.

# Using your Registered Retirement Savings Plan (RRSP) to finance real estate

Investments can be done through a strategy called a self-directed RRSP mortgage. Here's how it works:

1. Self-Directed RRSP: First, ensure that your RRSP is self-directed, meaning you have control over where you invest your retirement savings. Traditional RRSPs typically limit investment options to stocks, bonds, and mutual funds, but self-directed RRSPs allow for a broader range of investment choices, including real estate.

2. RRSP Mortgage: With a self-directed RRSP, you can lend money from your RRSP to finance a real estate purchase by issuing a mortgage. This means your RRSP becomes

the lender, and the borrower (usually yourself or a third party) pays back the loan with interest, just like a traditional mortgage from a bank.

3. Setting Up the Mortgage: To set up an RRSP mortgage, you'll need to work with a qualified mortgage administrator or trustee who specializes in self-directed RRSPs. They will help facilitate the transaction, ensure compliance with tax regulations, and handle the necessary paperwork.

4. Terms and Conditions: Determine the terms and conditions of the RRSP mortgage, including the loan amount, interest rate, repayment schedule, and collateral (the property being financed). These terms should be outlined in a legally binding mortgage agreement that protects both the borrower and the lender (your RRSP).

5. Tax Considerations: While RRSP withdrawals are typically taxed as income, there are tax advantages to using your RRSP to finance real estate investments. For example, the interest earned on the RRSP mortgage is tax-deferred as long as it remains within the RRSP. However, consult with a tax advisor to understand the specific tax implications based on your situation.

6. Repayment: As the borrower, you (or the third-party borrower) are responsible for repaying the RRSP mortgage according to the agreed-upon terms. This includes making regular payments of principal and interest to your RRSP, just like you would with a traditional mortgage from a financial institution.

7. Risk Management: While using your RRSP to finance real estate investments can be lucrative, it's essential to assess the risks involved. Ensure that the investment aligns

with your financial goals, conduct thorough due diligence on the property, and consider factors such as market conditions, rental income potential, and potential risks.

8.  Legal and Financial Advice: Before proceeding with an RRSP mortgage for real estate investing, seek advice from legal and financial professionals who specialize in self-directed RRSPs and real estate transactions. They can provide guidance tailored to your specific circumstances and help ensure compliance with regulations.

By leveraging your self-directed RRSP to finance real estate investments through an RRSP mortgage, you can diversify your retirement portfolio, potentially earn higher returns than traditional investment options, and take advantage of tax benefits associated with real estate investing. However, it's essential to approach this strategy with careful consideration, proper planning, and expert guidance.

Using your Registered Retirement Savings Plan (RRSP) to buy your first home is a smart strategy that can help you achieve homeownership while taking advantage of the tax benefits of your RRSP. Here's how it works:

1. Home Buyers' Plan (HBP): The Canadian government's Home Buyers' Plan (HBP) allows first-time homebuyers to withdraw up to $35,000 from their RRSP (or $70,000 for couples) to use towards the purchase of a qualifying home. To qualify as a first-time homebuyer, you must meet certain criteria, including not having owned a home in the past four years.

2. Eligible RRSPs: You can withdraw funds from any RRSP account that is registered in your name, as well as a spousal RRSP if you are the annuitant. However, you cannot withdraw

funds from a locked-in RRSP or a group RRSP.

3.  Repayment Requirement: The amount withdrawn from your RRSP under the HBP is considered a loan, and you must repay it to your RRSP over a period of up to 15 years. Repayments start the second year after the year of withdrawal. If you fail to make the required repayments, the amount not repaid will be included in your taxable income for that year.

4.  Withdrawal Process: To withdraw funds from your RRSP under the HBP, you must complete and submit Form T1036 (Home Buyers' Plan Request to Withdraw Funds) to your financial institution. You can withdraw funds directly or transfer them to a separate RRSP account designated for the HBP.

5. Use of Funds: The withdrawn funds can be used for various purposes related to buying or building a qualifying home, including the down payment, closing costs, land transfer taxes, legal fees, and certain other expenses.

6. Qualifying Home: To be eligible, the home you are purchasing or building must be located in Canada and intended to be your principal place of residence within one year of purchasing or building. It can be an existing home, a newly constructed home, or even a share in a co-operative housing corporation.

7. Tax Implications: While the withdrawals under the HBP are not subject to withholding tax, they are still considered taxable income, though you may not have to pay tax on the withdrawn amount if you meet certain conditions. Additionally, failing to repay the required amount to your RRSP can result in tax consequences.

8. Consultation and Planning: Before utilizing your RRSP under the Home Buyers' Plan, it's crucial to consult with a financial advisor or tax professional to understand the implications and ensure that it aligns with your overall financial plan.

By leveraging the Home Buyers' Plan, you can tap into your RRSP savings to fund the purchase of your first home, making homeownership more accessible while benefiting from the tax advantages of your RRSP. However, it's essential to approach this strategy thoughtfully and seek professional guidance to maximize its benefits and avoid potential pitfalls.

# Private Mortgages

Private mortgages, also known as private loans or private financing, are loans provided by individuals or private companies rather than traditional financial institutions like banks or credit unions. These lenders can include private investors, family members, or specialized lending firms.

Features of Private Mortgages:

1. Flexible Terms: Private mortgages often offer more flexibility in terms of loan amounts, repayment schedules, and eligibility criteria compared to traditional lenders.

2. Quick Approval: Private mortgage lenders typically have streamlined approval processes, allowing borrowers to access funds more quickly than with traditional lenders.

3. Credit Requirements: Private mortgage lenders may be more lenient with credit requirements, making them an option for borrowers with less-than-perfect credit scores.

4. Higher Interest Rates: Private mortgages usually come with higher interest rates compared to

conventional mortgages, reflecting the increased risk for the lender.

5. Shorter Terms: Private mortgages often have shorter terms, typically ranging from one to five years, although longer terms may be negotiated in some cases.

When to Use Private Mortgages:

- Credit Issues: Borrowers with poor credit histories who may not qualify for conventional mortgages may turn to private lenders for financing.

- Unique Properties: Properties that do not meet the criteria of traditional lenders, such as unique construction or unconventional locations, may be financed through private mortgages.

- Quick Financing: In situations where time is of the essence, such as purchasing a property at auction or completing a time-sensitive real estate transaction, private mortgages can provide quick access to funding.

- Investment Properties: Real estate investors looking to finance investment properties or renovation projects may turn to private mortgages for flexibility and speed of funding.

- Bridge Financing: Borrowers in need of short-term financing to bridge the gap between the purchase of a new property and the sale of an existing one may use private mortgages as interim financing.

Considerations:

- Higher Costs: Private mortgages often come with higher interest rates and fees compared to traditional mortgages, so borrowers should carefully consider the overall cost of borrowing.

- Exit Strategy: Borrowers should have a clear plan for repaying the loan, whether through refinancing with a traditional lender, selling the property, or other means.

- Risk: Both borrowers and lenders should assess the risks associated with private mortgages, including the potential for default, property depreciation, and legal complexities.

In summary, private mortgages can be a valuable financing option for borrowers who cannot access traditional bank financing or require quick, flexible funding for unique real estate transactions. However, borrowers should carefully weigh the benefits and risks and consider consulting with financial professionals before pursuing this financing option.

# Chapter 3; The Equity Game

## (How to use it and Make more money)

 Refinancing, or REFI, is a strategic move that allows homeowners to leverage their home equity for various financial goals. It involves replacing an existing mortgage with a new one, usually to take advantage of lower interest rates, access equity, or change the loan terms. Here's a breakdown of when to consider refinancing and how to maximize its benefits

**When to REFI?**

- Interest Rates Drop: Refinancing can be beneficial when interest rates decrease significantly, allowing you to secure a lower rate and potentially lower your monthly payments.
- Equity Accumulation: As your home's value increases and you build equity through mortgage payments, refinancing allows you to access that equity for other financial goals.
- Change in Financial Situation: If your financial circumstances change, such as a higher credit score or increased income, refinancing can help you qualify for better terms.

Timing of REFI:

- No Set Waiting Period: There's no specific waiting period required before refinancing after purchasing a home. However, some lenders may have their own guidelines, so it's essential to check with your lender.
- Consider Prepayment Penalties: If your existing mortgage has prepayment penalties, factor them into your decision-making process before refinancing.

Potential Proceeds:

- Loan-to-Value Ratio: The amount you can take out in a refinance depends on your home's appraised value and the lender's loan-to-value (LTV) ratio requirements. Typically, lenders allow you to borrow up to 80% of your home's appraised value, minus any existing mortgage balance.

- ETO (Equity Take Out) or Cash-Out Refinance: With a cash-out refinance, you can access a portion of your home's equity in the form of cash, which can be used for home improvements, debt consolidation, investments, or other expenses.

**Planning Considerations:**

- Financial Goals: Determine your financial objectives for refinancing, whether it's lowering your monthly payments, reducing your interest rate, accessing cash, or consolidating debt.
- Costs and Fees: Be aware of the closing costs associated with refinancing, including appraisal fees, origination fees, and title insurance. Compare these costs with the potential savings or benefits of refinancing.
- Long-Term Impact: Consider the long-term implications of refinancing, such as extending or shortening the loan term, and how it aligns with your overall financial strategy.

Affordability After REFI:

- Lower Monthly Payments: Refinancing to a lower interest rate or extending the loan term can result in reduced monthly mortgage payments, improving affordability.

- Debt Consolidation: If you use a cash-out refinance to consolidate high-interest debt, your overall monthly payments may decrease, improving your financial stability.

How It Works:

- Application Process: To refinance, you'll need to complete a new mortgage application, provide documentation of income and assets, and undergo a credit check.

- Appraisal: A new appraisal of your home will be conducted to determine its current market value, which impacts the amount you can borrow.

- Closing: Once approved, you'll sign the loan documents, pay any closing costs, and the new loan will replace your existing mortgage.

Getting the Best Deal:
- Shop Around: Compare rates and terms from multiple lenders to ensure you're getting the best deal. Consider working with a mortgage broker who can help you access a variety of loan options.

- Negotiate: Don't hesitate to negotiate with lenders to secure lower interest rates or reduced fees.

- Consider Points: Depending on your financial situation, paying discount points upfront in exchange for a lower interest rate may be beneficial.

In summary, refinancing can be a valuable financial tool when used strategically. By understanding when to refinance, considering timing, potential proceeds, planning considerations, affordability, and how to secure the best deal, homeowners can make informed decisions to maximize their financial goals.

# How to Play with your HELOC

A Home Equity Line of Credit (HELOC) isn't just another financial product; it's your ticket to flexible and strategic borrowing. Think of it as a financial Swiss Army knife, ready to handle a variety of needs and opportunities. Here's how to make the most out of your HELOC

Accessing Funds:

- HELOC Basics: A HELOC allows you to borrow against the equity in your home, similar to a credit card. The amount you can borrow is based on the equity you've built up in your home.
- Flexible Withdrawals: You can access funds from your HELOC as needed, up to your approved credit limit, making it a convenient source of financing for various expenses.

Leveraging Equity:

- Home Improvements: Use your HELOC to fund renovations or upgrades that can increase your home's value, such as a kitchen remodel or bathroom renovation.
- Debt Consolidation: Consolidate high-interest debt, such as credit card balances or personal

loans, into your HELOC to potentially lower your overall interest costs.

Interest Savings:

- Lower Interest Rates: HELOCs often have lower interest rates compared to credit cards or personal loans, making them a cost-effective option for borrowing.
- Interest-Only Payments: Some HELOCs offer the flexibility of making interest-only payments during the draw period, which can help manage cash flow.

Investment Opportunities:

- Real Estate Investments: Use funds from your HELOC to finance investment properties or real estate ventures, potentially generating additional income or building wealth through property appreciation.
- Stock Market Investments: Invest in stocks, bonds, or other investment vehicles using your HELOC funds to potentially earn higher returns than the interest rate on your HELOC.

Emergency Fund:

- Financial Safety Net: Keep a portion of your HELOC untapped as an emergency fund to cover unexpected expenses, such as medical bills or home repairs.
- Access to Cash: Having a HELOC in place provides quick access to funds in case of

emergencies, offering peace of mind during uncertain times.

Smart Repayment Strategies:

- Paying Down Principal: Aim to pay down the principal balance on your HELOC over time to reduce interest costs and build equity in your home.
- Budgeting for Payments: Create a repayment plan to ensure you can afford the monthly payments on your HELOC, especially if interest rates rise or your financial situation changes.

Monitoring Interest Rates:

- Interest Rate Changes: Keep an eye on interest rate trends and be prepared for potential changes in your HELOC's interest rate, especially if it has a variable rate.
- Refinancing Options: Consider refinancing your HELOC if you can secure a lower interest rate or better terms, potentially saving you money on interest payments.

Financial Discipline:

- Responsible Borrowing: Use your HELOC responsibly and avoid overextending yourself by borrowing more than you can afford to repay.
- Financial Planning: Incorporate your HELOC into your overall financial plan and use it as a tool to achieve your financial goals, whether it's paying

for education, funding retirement, or purchasing a second home.

By understanding how to play with your HELOC and using it wisely, you can unlock its potential to finance your goals, save on interest costs, and build wealth over time. However, it's essential to approach HELOC borrowing with caution and discipline to avoid financial pitfalls and ensure long-term financial stability.

## Put you Mortgage into a Blender

**Refinancing with a "Blend and Extend" strategy is like giving your mortgage a refreshing new twist. This approach combines your existing mortgage rate with current market rates while extending the term of your loan, potentially easing your financial load. Here's a breakdown of how it works and why you might want to consider it**

Blend and Extend Process:

Blend: The term "blend" refers to combining your existing mortgage rate with the current market rate. Your lender will calculate a blended rate based on the remaining balance of your current mortgage and the prevailing market rate.

Extend: The term "extend" involves extending the term of your mortgage. By refinancing, you can reset the clock on your mortgage term, potentially reducing your monthly payments.

Reasons to Consider Blend and Extend:

Lower Monthly Payments: By blending your existing mortgage rate with the current market rate and extending the term, you may be able to reduce your monthly mortgage payments, providing relief for your budget.

Cash Flow Management: Lower monthly payments can improve your cash flow and provide flexibility in managing your finances. This extra cash can be redirected towards other expenses or investments.

Interest Savings: Depending on market conditions and the difference between your existing rate and the current rate, blending and extending could lead to interest savings over the life of the loan.

Stability and Predictability: Extending the term of your mortgage can provide stability and predictability in your housing costs by locking in a fixed monthly payment for an extended period.

Factors to Consider:

Overall Cost: While blend and extend can reduce your monthly payments, it's essential to consider the overall cost of refinancing, including closing costs and any prepayment penalties associated with your existing mortgage.

Long-Term Goals: Assess whether the potential monthly savings outweigh the additional interest costs over the extended term. Consider your long-term financial goals and whether blend and extend aligns with your objectives.

Market Conditions: Monitor current interest rates and market trends to determine if blend and extend makes sense given prevailing economic conditions. Consult with your lender or financial advisor for personalized guidance.

How to Proceed:

Evaluate Your Options: Review your current mortgage terms, including interest rate, remaining balance, and term. Compare these with current market rates and projected monthly payments under a blend and extend scenario.

Consult with Your Lender: Schedule a meeting with your lender to discuss the blend and extend option and assess its suitability based on your financial situation and goals. Your lender can provide personalized advice and assist you in navigating the refinancing process.

Review the Terms: Carefully review the terms and conditions of the refinanced mortgage, including any changes to the interest rate, term, and closing costs. Ensure you understand the implications of blend and extend before proceeding.

Refinancing with a "Blend and Extend" approach can be a powerful tool for homeowners looking to lower their monthly payments, improve cash flow, and gain financial flexibility. However, it's essential to weigh the potential benefits against the long-term costs and align this strategy with your overall financial objectives. Consulting with a lender or financial advisor will help ensure you make an informed decision that's right for you

# Chapter 4; The Investors' Exclusive Arena

**In the fast-paced world of real estate investing, the array of mortgage products available to investors is both vast and tailored to meet specific needs. Whether you're flipping homes, expanding your rental portfolio, or diving into commercial real estate, there's likely a mortgage product designed just for you. Let's explore some investor-centric mortgage options and understand why the market is rich with such choices**

1. Purchase Plus Improvement Mortgages:

What They Are: Purchase plus improvement mortgages are tailored for investors looking to purchase a property that requires renovations or upgrades. These mortgages provide financing not only for the purchase price of the property but also for the cost of approved improvements.
Why They Exist: These mortgages cater to investors seeking to add value to their properties and increase

their investment returns. By bundling the purchase and renovation costs into a single mortgage, investors can streamline the financing process and access the capital needed to enhance the property's value.


## 2. Readvanceable Mortgages:

What They Are: Readvanceable mortgages, also known as home equity lines of credit (HELOCs), allow investors to access the equity in their properties as a revolving line of credit. As the mortgage principal is paid down or the property appreciates in value, the available credit limit increases, providing ongoing access to funds.
Why They Exist: These mortgages offer flexibility and liquidity to investors, enabling them to leverage their equity for various purposes such as renovations, property acquisitions, or investment opportunities. Readvanceable mortgages empower investors to unlock the value of their real estate holdings without the need for additional financing.


## 3. Cash Back Mortgages:

What They Are: Cash back mortgages provide borrowers with a lump sum cash payment upon closing, typically calculated as a percentage of the mortgage amount. This cash can be used for various purposes, including covering closing costs, renovations, or as additional capital for investments.

Why They Exist: Cash back mortgages appeal to investors seeking to offset upfront expenses or bolster their cash reserves. By receiving a cash injection at the outset, investors can enhance their financial flexibility and seize investment opportunities without depleting their savings.

## 4. Open Mortgages:

What They Are: Open mortgages offer borrowers the flexibility to repay the mortgage principal in part or in full at any time without incurring prepayment penalties. These mortgages typically have higher interest rates than closed mortgages but provide greater flexibility and freedom.
Why They Exist: Open mortgages cater to investors who prioritize flexibility and wish to capitalize on short-term investment opportunities or unforeseen changes in their financial circumstances. Investors can take advantage of open mortgages to make lump sum payments, refinance, or sell properties without being bound by restrictive prepayment terms.

Why the Industry is Full of Products:
The real estate investment landscape is dynamic and diverse, with investors having unique goals, risk tolerances, and financial profiles. Mortgage lenders continually innovate and introduce new products to meet the evolving needs of investors and provide tailored solutions for various investment strategies. By offering a

range of specialized mortgage products, lenders empower investors to optimize their financing strategies, unlock value from their real estate holdings, and achieve their investment objectives with confidence.

In essence, the abundance of investor-centric mortgage products reflects the dynamism and vibrancy of the real estate investment market, providing investors with the tools and resources they need to thrive in their pursuit of financial success.

## Sarah's Journey: A Tale of Bold Moves in Real Estate

In the bustling world of real estate investing, there was Sarah—a visionary with a keen eye for potential and an unyielding drive to succeed. Sarah wasn't satisfied with the mundane; she sought the extraordinary. Her journey began modestly, with a single investment property, but her ambitions reached far beyond the ordinary.

Sarah scoured the market, always on the lookout for hidden opportunities. One day, she discovered a diamond in the rough—an aging property brimming with potential but desperately in need of a makeover. Where others saw obstacles, Sarah saw a golden opportunity.

Determined to bring her vision to life, Sarah knew traditional financing wouldn't suffice for such a bold project. She turned to the Purchase Plus Improvement Mortgage—a perfect match for her ambitious plan. This specialized loan provided the funds needed to buy the property and finance the extensive renovations.

The months that followed were a whirlwind. Sarah threw herself into the renovation project, transforming the neglected property into a stunning masterpiece. Her dedication and creative vision paid off, breathing new life into the old structure and significantly boosting its value.

But Sarah's journey didn't stop there. Riding high on her initial success, she continued to push boundaries in the real estate market. She explored innovative financing options like Readvanceable Mortgages and Cash Back Mortgages, leveraging them to seize new opportunities and expand her portfolio.

With each new investment, Sarah's confidence grew. Her reputation as a savvy investor spread, inspiring others in the industry. She demonstrated that with courage, creativity, and a willingness to embrace unconventional solutions, anything was possible.

Today, Sarah stands tall among the giants of real estate. Her portfolio is a testament to her boldness and ingenuity. Her story is a powerful reminder that in the world of investing, fortune favors the bold. Those who dare to dream big and act on it.

## and taking calculated risks are destined for Excellence.

# Chapter 5;
# MULTIFAMILY

This chapter is named Multifamily as it was inspired by the Multifamily Conference the biggest real estate conference in Toronto by Seth Furguson. I am not paid for promoting this conference in fact I am not paid for any mentions in this book. I only share what I think is valuable and I am committed to protect my credibility throughout this book. I do so as a personal choice. Let's Learn.

What You Need to Know About Bigger than Fourplexes ?

Investing in multifamily properties larger than fourplexes presents unique opportunities and considerations for real estate investors. Here's what you need to know about these larger multifamily properties:

Scale and Income Potential:

- Properties larger than fourplexes typically offer greater scale, with five or more units, translating to higher rental income potential.
- The increased number of units allows for diversified income streams, reducing the impact of vacancies and maximizing cash flow.

Financing Options:

- Financing for multifamily properties larger than fourplexes may fall under commercial lending or specialized multifamily mortgages.
- Lenders may offer loans with terms and conditions tailored to the specific needs of larger multifamily buildings, considering factors such as property size, rental income, and market conditions.

Management Requirements:

- Managing larger multifamily properties requires efficient organization and oversight.
- Investors may choose to hire professional property management companies to handle day-to-day operations, tenant relations, and maintenance tasks.

Market Dynamics:

- Market demand for multifamily properties larger than fourplexes can vary depending on location, population density, and rental market trends.
- Urban areas or regions with strong job growth and limited housing supply often present favorable conditions for investing in larger multifamily buildings.

Regulatory Considerations:

- Zoning regulations and local ordinances may impose restrictions on the use and development of larger multifamily properties.
- Investors should familiarize themselves with zoning laws, building codes, and permitting requirements to ensure compliance and avoid potential issues.

Due Diligence:

- Conducting thorough due diligence is essential when investing in multifamily properties larger than fourplexes.

- This includes assessing the property's condition, rental history, operating expenses, and potential for future appreciation.

- Financial analysis should consider factors such as rental income, vacancy rates, property taxes, insurance, and maintenance costs to determine the property's investment viability.

Long-Term Investment Strategy:

- Investing in multifamily properties larger than fourplexes is often part of a long-term wealth-building strategy.
- Investors should consider their investment goals, risk tolerance, and exit strategy when acquiring larger multifamily properties, aiming to generate passive income and build equity over time.

In summary, investing in multifamily properties larger than fourplexes offers investors the potential for increased rental income and long-term wealth accumulation. By understanding the scale, financing options, management requirements, market dynamics, regulatory considerations, due diligence, and long-term investment strategy associated with larger multifamily properties, investors can make informed decisions and capitalize on opportunities in the multifamily real estate market.

# Debt Coverage Ratio DCR

When it comes to multifamily properties with five or more units, the Debt Coverage Ratio (DCR) becomes a pivotal metric. Here's why understanding DCR is essential for investors in larger multifamily properties

Debt Coverage Ratio (DCR) is a critical metric in multifamily investing, especially for properties larger than four units. Here's how DCR applies in multifamily investing and why it's essential for properties with five or more units:

Understanding DCR:

- DCR is a measure of a property's ability to generate enough income to cover its debt obligations, specifically the mortgage payments.
- It is calculated by dividing the property's Net Operating Income (NOI) by its total debt service (mortgage payments).

Importance in Multifamily Investing:

- For multifamily properties, lenders typically require a minimum DCR to qualify for financing.

- DCR provides lenders with assurance that the property's rental income is sufficient to cover mortgage payments, reducing the risk of default.

Considerations for Properties with Five or More Units:

- Larger multifamily properties often have more complex operating expenses and income streams compared to smaller properties.
- DCR becomes even more critical for properties with five or more units due to the scale of operations and financing involved.

Calculating DCR:

- To calculate DCR, first determine the property's NOI, which is the total rental income minus operating expenses (property taxes, insurance, utilities, maintenance, management fees, etc.).
- Then, divide the NOI by the property's total debt service, including principal and interest payments on the mortgage.

Minimum DCR Requirements:

- Lenders typically require a minimum DCR of 1.2 to 1.3 for multifamily properties.
- A DCR of 1.2 means that the property's net operating income is 20% higher than its debt service, providing a cushion for unexpected expenses or vacancies.

Implications for Financing:

- A higher DCR indicates greater financial stability and reduces the lender's risk, potentially leading to more favorable loan terms and lower interest rates.
- Properties with lower DCR may require larger down payments or higher interest rates to mitigate the lender's risk.

Monitoring DCR:

- DCR should be monitored regularly to ensure the property remains financially healthy and can continue to meet its debt obligations.
- Changes in rental income, operating expenses, or interest rates can impact DCR and may require adjustments to the property's management or financing strategy.

In summary, Debt Coverage Ratio (DCR) is a fundamental metric in multifamily investing, particularly for properties with five or more units. Investors should understand how DCR is calculated, its importance in securing financing, and its implications for property profitability and financial stability. By maintaining a healthy DCR, investors can mitigate risks and maximize the long-term success of their multifamily investments. Embracing the Debt Coverage Ratio (DCR) as a key metric ensures financial stability and paves the way for successful multifamily investments. Like Sarah, investors who leverage these insights can confidently navigate the multifamily landscape and achieve their investment goals.

# Income in a Multi Family investing?

In multifamily investing, the focus shifts from individual creditworthiness to the financial performance and potential of the property. Here's a detailed look at the key differences between residential and multifamily investing and why multifamily properties can be a lucrative venture

While personal credit plays a significant role in residential investing, multifamily investing places greater **emphasis on the property's financial performance** and potential but don't forget that still the personal credit and standing is a factor. Here are some other key differences between residential and multifamily investing:

- **Scale**: Multifamily properties typically involve larger scale investments compared to residential properties. Instead of purchasing individual homes, investors acquire buildings with multiple units, which can range from small apartment complexes to large-scale developments.

- **Income Potential**: Multifamily properties offer greater income potential due to multiple rental units within a single property. This diversified income stream can provide more stable cash flow and mitigate risks associated with vacancies or tenant turnover.

- **Professional Management**: Managing multifamily properties often requires more specialized skills and resources compared to residential properties. Many investors opt to hire professional property management companies to oversee operations, tenant relations, and maintenance.

- **Financing:** Financing for multifamily properties differs from residential properties in terms of eligibility criteria, loan terms, and down payment requirements. Lenders assess the property's income-generating potential and use metrics like Debt Coverage Ratio (DCR) to evaluate loan eligibility.

- **Market Dynamics:** Multifamily real estate operates within its own market dynamics, which may be influenced by factors such as job growth, population density, and rental demand.

Understanding these market dynamics is essential for successful multifamily investing.

- Value Appreciation: While both residential and multifamily properties can appreciate in value over time, multifamily properties may offer additional value appreciation potential through strategic renovations, improved management, and increasing rental income.

- Risk Management: Multifamily investing involves unique risks, such as tenant turnover, economic downturns affecting rental demand, and regulatory changes affecting landlord-tenant laws. Investors must implement effective risk management strategies to mitigate these risks and protect their investment.

- Exit Strategies: Exit strategies for multifamily investments may differ from residential properties and can include options such as selling the property as-is, renovating and increasing rents, or refinancing to leverage equity for additional investments.

Overall, multifamily investing offers distinct opportunities and challenges compared to residential investing, requiring a tailored approach and understanding of the multifamily market dynamics. While personal credit may be less critical in multifamily investing, investors must focus on property performance, market analysis, and effective management to maximize returns and build long-term wealth.

## Corporations;

**The majority of multifamily buildings in Ontario are typically acquired through individual ownership or limited liability companies (LLCs), which are referred to as corporations in Canada. These ownership structures offer investors flexibility, control, and liability protection. However, partnerships and real estate investment trusts (REITs) also play a significant role in the multifamily real estate market, providing investors with alternative avenues for investment and diversification. Ultimately, the choice of ownership structure depends on the investor's preferences, objectives, and risk tolerance.**

Understanding Appraisal, Inspection, and Environmental Assessment Costs in Multifamily Investing

Appraisal, inspection, and environmental assessment are essential steps in the due diligence process when investing in multifamily properties. Let's delve into the costs associated with these assessments:

Appraisal Costs:

- Purpose: An appraisal determines the fair market value of the property, ensuring that the purchase price aligns with its worth.
- Cost Range: Appraisal fees vary depending on factors such as property size, location, complexity, and the appraiser's credentials. Costs typically range from $500 to $1,500 or more for multifamily properties.
- Importance: Appraisals provide lenders with assurance regarding the property's value, influencing loan approval and terms. Investors rely on accurate appraisals to assess investment potential and negotiate purchase prices.

Inspection Costs:

- Purpose: Property inspections assess the condition of the building, identifying any structural issues, safety concerns, or necessary repairs.
- Cost Range: Inspection fees vary based on property size, age, and the extent of inspection services required. Costs for multifamily properties typically range from $300 to $1,000 or more.
- Importance: Inspections help investors uncover hidden defects or maintenance issues that may affect the property's value, rental income, and future expenses. Addressing inspection findings informs negotiation strategies and renovation plans.

Environmental Assessment Costs:

- Purpose: Environmental assessments evaluate the property for potential environmental hazards or contamination, such as soil or water pollution, hazardous materials, or regulatory violations.
- Cost Range: Environmental assessment costs depend on factors such as property size, location, historical land use, and the scope of assessment required. Costs can

range from $1,500 to $5,000 or more for multifamily properties.

- Importance: Environmental assessments mitigate risks associated with liability, regulatory compliance, and remediation costs. Identifying environmental issues early in the due diligence process allows investors to factor potential liabilities into their investment decision-making and negotiate appropriate terms.

Budgeting and Planning:

- Consideration: While appraisal, inspection, and environmental assessment costs are necessary for due diligence, investors should budget for these expenses as part of the overall acquisition costs.
- Financial Impact: Allocating funds for assessments upfront can prevent surprises and ensure thorough evaluation of the property's condition and risks.
- Professional Guidance: Working with experienced appraisers, inspectors, and environmental consultants is essential for obtaining accurate assessments and actionable insights.

By understanding and planning for these costs, investors can conduct thorough due diligence, mitigate risks, and make informed decisions that maximize the potential returns of their multifamily properties

# Chapter 6; Don't fall for it!

The first and the most and the biggest mistake is taking on the wrong financing at first purchase. DON'T DO IT!

Taking on the wrong financing at the first purchase can indeed be a significant and costly mistake in real estate investing. Here's why:

1. Impact on Cash Flow: Choosing the wrong financing option, such as a high-interest loan or an unfavorable mortgage structure, can significantly impact cash flow. Higher monthly payments or unexpected expenses can erode profitability and make it challenging to cover operating costs, maintenance, or vacancies.
2. Long-Term Commitment: Real estate financing often involves long-term commitments, such as mortgages with

terms ranging from 15 to 30 years. Committing to the wrong financing option at the outset can lock investors into unfavorable terms, limiting flexibility and hindering future investment opportunities.

3. Limited Investment Capacity: Inflexible or high-cost financing may limit an investor's capacity to acquire additional properties or pursue growth opportunities. Suboptimal financing terms can reduce borrowing capacity, increase debt-to-income ratios, or restrict access to capital for future investments.

4. Impact on ROI: The choice of financing directly affects the return on investment (ROI) of a real estate investment. High-interest rates, excessive fees, or unfavorable loan terms can diminish potential returns and reduce overall profitability, undermining the investment's financial viability.

5. Financial Risk: Taking on the wrong financing exposes investors to financial risk, such as default, foreclosure, or bankruptcy. Inadequate capital reserves, insufficient cash flow, or unfavorable loan terms can increase

the likelihood of financial distress and jeopardize the investment's success.

**To dodge these pitfalls, make sure to conduct thorough research and financial analysis. Consult with professionals like mortgage brokers or real estate attorneys to guide you through the process and align your financing with your goals"**

The 2nd Biggest Mistake in Real Estate Investing: Failing to Perform Due Diligence

Real estate investing offers tremendous potential for wealth creation, but it also carries inherent risks. Among the myriad of potential pitfalls, perhaps the most significant mistake investors can make is failing to conduct thorough due diligence. Here's why:

Inadequate Market Research:

Problem: Investing in a market without understanding its dynamics, trends, and economic fundamentals can lead to poor investment decisions. Lack of market research may result in investing in areas with declining property values, low rental demand, or unfavorable economic conditions.
Solution: Prioritize comprehensive market research to identify promising investment opportunities. Analyze factors such as population growth, employment trends, infrastructure developments, and rental demand to assess the viability of the market.
Lack of Property Analysis:

Problem: Investing in a property without thoroughly evaluating its physical condition, potential risks, and investment potential can lead to unforeseen expenses and challenges. Ignoring property inspections or neglecting to assess renovation or maintenance needs can result in costly repairs or vacancies.

Solution: Conduct detailed property inspections, assessments, and evaluations to identify any issues or red flags. Hire qualified professionals, such as home inspectors, engineers, or contractors, to assess the property's condition, structural integrity, and renovation requirements.

**Ignoring Financial Analysis:**

Problem: Failing to perform comprehensive financial analysis can result in overpaying for a property, underestimating expenses, or miscalculating potential returns. Ignoring cash flow projections, financing costs, or operating expenses can lead to negative cash flow or inadequate returns on investment.
Solution: Conduct thorough financial analysis, including cash flow projections, income analysis, expense forecasting, and return on investment calculations. Consider all expenses, such as mortgage payments, property taxes, insurance, maintenance, vacancies, and property management fees, to accurately assess the property's financial performance.
Underestimating Risks:

Problem: Neglecting to identify and mitigate potential risks associated with real estate investments can result in financial losses or investment failure. Ignoring risks such as market volatility, tenant turnover, regulatory changes, or environmental hazards can expose investors to unforeseen challenges.

Solution: Conduct a comprehensive risk assessment to identify and mitigate potential risks. Consider factors such as property location, market conditions, tenant quality, lease agreements, insurance coverage, and legal compliance to proactively address potential risks and minimize their impact on investment outcomes.

Rushing Into Investments:

Problem: Succumbing to pressure or rushing into investments without adequate research or analysis can lead to impulsive decisions and poor investment outcomes. Failing to take the time to conduct due diligence and fully understand the investment can result in costly mistakes.

Solution: Exercise patience and discipline when evaluating investment opportunities. Take the time to thoroughly research, analyze, and assess each potential investment before making a decision. Consider seeking advice from experienced professionals or mentors to gain valuable insights and perspective.

In summary, failing to perform due diligence is perhaps the biggest mistake an investor can make in real estate investing. By prioritizing thorough market research, property analysis, financial assessment, risk mitigation, and disciplined decision-making, investors can avoid costly mistakes and maximize their chances of success in the dynamic world of real estate investing.

## Major Miss Step: Making an offer without talking to your Trusted Mortgage broker

**Avoid this Huge Mistake,** Making an offer on a property without consulting your mortgage broker can indeed lead to significant challenges and missed opportunities in real estate investing. Here's why it's crucial to involve your mortgage broker in the early stages of the property purchase process:

1. Understanding Affordability: Your mortgage broker can assess your financial situation, including your income, assets, debts, and credit history, to determine how much you can afford to borrow. This information is essential for establishing a realistic budget and making informed decisions about property affordability.

2. Pre-Approval Process: Obtaining a pre-approval from your mortgage broker before making an offer provides you with a clear understanding of your borrowing capacity and strengthens your negotiating position. Sellers are more likely to consider offers from pre-approved buyers, as they demonstrate seriousness and financial readiness.

3. Identifying Financing Options: Your mortgage broker can explore various financing options tailored to your needs and preferences, such as different loan programs, down payment requirements, and interest rate structures. This ensures that you choose the most suitable financing solution for your investment goals and financial situation.

4. Evaluating Offer Terms: Your mortgage broker can review the terms of the purchase offer, including financing contingencies, down payment amounts, and closing timelines, to ensure they align with your financing requirements and objectives. This helps minimize the risk of encountering financing-related issues during the transaction process.

5. Avoiding Surprises: By involving your mortgage broker early on, you can anticipate and address any potential financing challenges or obstacles upfront. This proactive approach helps prevent last-minute surprises, delays, or deal-breaking issues that could jeopardize the transaction.

6. Strategic Planning: Your mortgage broker can provide valuable insights and advice on structuring your offer to enhance its competitiveness while maintaining financial prudence. This may include strategies such as including escalation clauses, adjusting financing terms, or offering a larger down payment to strengthen your offer.

Overall, consulting with your mortgage broker before making an offer on a property empowers you to make informed decisions, maximize your financing options, and streamline the transaction process. Their expertise and guidance can help you navigate the complexities of real estate financing with confidence and achieve your investment objectives effectively.

# Proactive versus reactive financing

This represents two distinct approaches to managing your finances, particularly in the context of real estate investing. Here's how they differ:

Proactive Financing:

- Proactive financing involves taking a strategic and forward-thinking approach to managing your finances and investments.
- Investors who adopt a proactive approach actively seek out financing options - that align with their long-term goals and investment strategies.
- They anticipate future needs and plan ahead to secure the most favorable financing terms and opportunities.
- Proactive investors regularly review their financial situation, explore new financing options, and adjust their strategies based on changing market conditions.

By being proactive, investors can capitalize on favorable market conditions, maximize investment returns, and mitigate risks associated with unexpected financial challenges.

Reactive Financing:

- Reactive financing, on the other hand, involves responding to immediate financial needs or challenges as they arise.
- Investors who take a reactive approach may wait until they encounter a specific financing need or problem before seeking out solutions.
- They may be more inclined to react to market fluctuations, interest rate changes, or unexpected expenses rather than proactively planning for them.
- Reactive investors may miss out on opportunities to optimize their financing terms, secure better rates, or explore alternative financing options due to a lack of foresight and planning.
- While reactive financing can address immediate needs, it may result in higher costs, missed opportunities, or increased financial stress in the long run.

In the context of real estate investing, adopting a proactive financing approach is generally advisable as it allows investors to:

- Identify and secure financing options that best align with their investment goals and risk tolerance.
- Anticipate and plan for future financing needs, such as property acquisitions, renovations, or market fluctuations.
- Take advantage of favorable financing terms, interest rates, and investment opportunities before they become less favorable.
- Minimize the impact of unforeseen financial challenges or market downturns by having a well-thought-out financing strategy in place.

Overall, proactive financing empowers investors to take control of their financial future, optimize their investment returns, and navigate the complexities of real estate investing with confidence and foresight.

**BIG Mistake!**

It's very surprising that PEOPLE Think shopping for the best rate and believing that's the only thing that they need to care about and that's the only thing that makes them money. IT'S NOT TRUE

Indeed, that's a common misconception among some investors. While securing a competitive interest rate is undoubtedly important, focusing solely on finding the lowest rate can be a mistake. Here's why:

1. Incomplete Picture: A low interest rate might seem appealing on the surface, but it's just one piece of the financing puzzle. Other factors, such as loan terms, flexibility, prepayment penalties, and overall loan structure, can significantly impact the total cost of financing and the profitability of your investment.

2. Total Cost of Financing: A slightly higher interest rate with more favorable terms and fewer fees may ultimately result in lower overall financing costs than a loan with a lower rate but less favorable terms. It's essential to consider the total cost of financing over the life of the loan, including both interest payments and associated fees.

3. Risk Management: Opting for the lowest rate without considering other factors could expose you to additional risks. For example, a loan with strict prepayment penalties or limited flexibility may restrict your ability to refinance or sell the property if market conditions change.

4. Value-Add Opportunities: Sometimes, financing options with slightly higher rates may offer additional benefits, such as faster approval processes, higher leverage, or access to value-add features like renovation financing or cash-out refinancing. These features can enable you to maximize the potential return on your investment.

5. Long-Term Strategy: Real estate investing is inherently a long-term game, and your financing strategy should align with your investment goals and overall wealth-building

strategy. While securing the lowest rate may provide short-term savings, it's crucial to consider how your financing decisions will impact your investment portfolio and financial goals over the long term.

In summary, while securing a competitive interest rate is important, it's just one factor to consider when evaluating financing options for real estate investments. Taking a holistic approach, considering the total cost of financing, assessing risk factors, and aligning your financing strategy with your long-term investment objectives are essential steps in maximizing the profitability and success of your real estate ventures.

Taking advice from wrong people and very close people to you. People who have done nothing themselves

That's an astute observation. Seeking advice from those who lack experience or expertise in real estate investing can indeed lead to misguided decisions. Here's why relying on advice from inexperienced or ill-informed individuals can be risky:

1. Limited Perspective: Someone who hasn't been actively involved in real estate investing may lack a comprehensive understanding of the market dynamics, financing options, risk management strategies, and other critical factors that influence investment success. Their advice may be based on assumptions, hearsay, or outdated information, rather than real-world experience.

2. Biased or Misinformed Advice: Well-meaning friends or family members may offer advice based on their own personal biases, preferences, or limited understanding of your specific financial goals and risk tolerance. Their recommendations may not align with your investment objectives or the realities of the real estate market.

3. Risk of Overconfidence or Complacency: If you rely solely on advice from individuals who haven't achieved success in real estate investing themselves, you may inadvertently adopt a misguided sense of confidence or

complacency about your investment decisions. This false sense of security can lead to overlooking potential risks or failing to conduct thorough due diligence.

4. Potential for Conflict of Interest: In some cases, friends or family members may have their own agendas or interests that influence the advice they provide. Their recommendations may be influenced by factors unrelated to your best interests, such as personal relationships, financial incentives, or speculative beliefs.

5. Lack of Accountability: Unlike professional advisors or mentors with a track record of success in real estate investing, friends or family members may not be held accountable for the advice they offer. If their recommendations result in negative outcomes for your investments, there may be limited recourse or accountability.

To mitigate the risks associated with relying on advice from inexperienced or ill-informed individuals, consider the following:

- Seek Advice from Qualified Professionals: Consult with experienced real estate professionals, such as mortgage brokers, real estate agents, financial advisors, or seasoned investors, who can offer informed guidance based on their expertise and track record of success.
- Conduct Independent Research: Take the time to educate yourself about real estate investing principles, market trends, financing options, and risk management strategies. Conduct independent research and seek out reputable sources of information to inform your investment decisions.
- Exercise Critical Thinking: Evaluate the advice you receive critically, considering the source, credibility, and potential biases or motivations behind the recommendations. Don't hesitate to ask questions, challenge assumptions, and seek clarification before making investment decisions.
- Build a Network of Mentors: Surround yourself with experienced mentors and peers who have achieved success in real estate investing and are willing to share their insights, lessons learned, and best practices. Engage with local real estate investment

groups, attend networking events, and seek out mentorship opportunities to expand your knowledge and perspective.

By being discerning about the advice you receive and seeking guidance from qualified professionals and mentors, you can make more informed decisions and increase your likelihood of success in real estate investing.

# Chapter 7
# ASK QUESTIONS

Questions investors ask; fix or variable? When will I hit a

financing/mortgage wall? How to finance a US Property from Canada?

## Here's a breakdown;

Let's break it down and chop it up.

### 1. Fixed or Variable Rate Mortgage?
This decision depends on various factors, including your risk tolerance, market

conditions, and financial goals. Fixed-rate mortgages offer stability and predictability, with consistent monthly payments over the term of the loan. <u>Variable-rate mortgages, on the other hand, may initially offer lower interest rates but are subject to fluctuations based on market conditions. Consider factors such as your long-term investment strategy, the current interest rate environment, and your ability to tolerate potential fluctuations </u>in interest rates when choosing between fixed and variable rate mortgages. HOWEVER VARIABLE is INVESTORS FRIEND ALL DAY LONG!

2. When Will I Hit a Financing/Mortgage Wall? This question relates to your borrowing capacity and how it may evolve over time as you expand your real estate investment portfolio. It's essential to understand your lender's lending criteria, including debt-to-income ratios, loan-to-value ratios, and other factors that may impact your ability to secure

financing for future property acquisitions. Working with a knowledgeable mortgage broker can help you anticipate potential financing challenges and develop a strategic plan to overcome them.

3. Financing a US Real Estate from Canada: Financing a US real estate investment from Canada involves navigating cross-border lending requirements, currency exchange considerations, and legal complexities. You'll need to work with lenders who specialize in international real estate financing and understand the unique challenges and opportunities associated with transnational investments. Additionally, you'll need to consider factors such as foreign exchange risk, tax implications, and legal requirements when structuring your financing arrangements. Consulting with professionals who have expertise in cross-border real estate transactions can help you navigate these complexities and make informed decisions about financing your US real estate investment.

Each of these questions underscores the importance of careful planning, thorough research, and informed decision-making when it comes to real estate investing. By seeking guidance from knowledgeable professionals, staying abreast of market trends, and continuously evaluating your investment strategy, you can navigate the complexities of real estate financing and position yourself for long-term success in the property market.

# RED FLAGs

## Fraud Warning Signs or Red Flags

While there are many potential warning signs (often referred to as red flags) for mortgage fraud, some are more obvious than others. It is necessary for the mortgage agent to watch for these warning signs and complete proper due diligence if any of these warning signs are present. Of course, warning signs are not necessarily an indicator of mortgage fraud, but may be, and therefore should always be investigated.

## Identity

- The applicant cannot provide any photo identification or says that they will provide photo identification but consistently does not. The quality of the identification must also be considered, especially if it does not appear to be genuine.
- If the applicants are not available to meet or if one applicant is never present.
- If a Power of Attorney is being used, especially on behalf of a senior

## Employment and Income

- The applicant's job letter contains inconsistencies or errors. (e.g., if it does not match pay stubs or what the applicant has disclosed about the amount of income, the time employed or their job title or has spelling or grammatical errors).
- If, when verifying the applicant's employment, the broker/agent cannot find a directory listing for the business, or the business contact number (as provided or as stated on the job letter) is a residential number or cellular number. This information can be obtained by conducting a business phone number search or reverse directory lookup using www.canada411.ca or other Internet services. Google is the best for this.
- The position and/or income are inconsistent with the applicant's age
- Employment verifications addressed to a specific party's attention
- Employment verifications completed on the same day they were ordered
- Employment verifications on a weekend or holiday
- Documentation which includes deletions, correction fluid, or other alterations
- Numbers on the documentation appear to be "squeezed" due to alteration
- Different handwriting or type styles within a document

- Employer's address is a post office box, the property address, or applicant's current residence
- Applicant's residence is (will be) in a location remote from employer
- Employer's name is similar to a party to the transaction, (g., utilizes applicant's initials)
- Employer is unable to be contacted
- Year-to-date or past-year earnings are even dollar amounts
- Withholding is not calculated correctly
- Withholding totals don't increase from pay stub to pay stub
- Pay period dates overlap and/or don't correspond with other documentation
- Abnormalities in pay cheque numbering
- Handwritten paystubs
- Income appears to be out of line with type of employment
- Self-employed applicant does not make estimated tax payments
- Real estate taxes or mortgage interest claimed, but no ownership of real property disclosed
- Tax returns not signed or dated
- High income applicant without tax return preparer
- Paid preparer signs taxpayer's copy of tax returns
- Interest and dividend income don't substantiate assets

- Applicant reports substantial income but has no cash in bank
- Reasonableness test: income appears to be out of line with type of employment, applicant age, education and/or lifestyle

## Assets

- The applicant states that they have significant income but little or no assets.
- Down payment source is other than deposits (gift, sale of personal property)
- Applicant's salary doesn't support savings on deposit
- Applicant doesn't utilize traditional banking institutions
- Pattern of loyalty to financial institutions other than the subject lender
- Balances are greater than the Canadian Deposit Insurance Corporation (CDIC) insured limits
- High asset applicant's investments are not diversified
- Excessive balance maintained in checking account
- Dates of bank statements are unusual or out of sequence
- Recently deposited funds without a plausible paper-trail or explanation
- Bank account ownership includes unknown parties
- Balances verified as even dollar amounts

- Source of earnest/deposit money is not apparent
- Earnest/deposit money isn't reflected in account withdrawals
- Earnest/deposit money is from a bank or account with no relationship to the applicant
- Bank statements do not reflect deposits consistent with income
- Reasonableness Test: Assets appear to be out of line with type of employment, applicant age, education and/or lifestyle

## Meeting Location

- If the client insists on meeting at a location other than the location of the property to be mortgaged. This may simply be based on convenience, and if the broker/agent's process includes meeting in their office this may not be considered a warning sign. The broker/agent should request a copy of a recent utility bill with the applicant's address and name.

## Contact Information

- If the applicant only has a cellular phone for contact purposes (although more consumers are using cellular phones as their homes phone).

- Same telephone number for applicant and employer

## Purchase and Sale Agreement

- Non arms-length transaction: seller is a real estate broker, relative, employer, etc.
- Seller is not currently reflected on title
- Purchaser is not the applicant
- Purchaser(s) deleted from/added to sales contract
- No real estate agent is involved
- Power of Attorney is used
- Second mortgage is indicated, but not disclosed on the application
- Earnest/deposit money equals the entire down payment, or is an odd amount
- Multiple deposit cheques have inconsistent dates, g., #303 dated 10/1, #299 dated 11/1
- Name and/or address on earnest/deposit money cheque differ from buyer
- Real estate commission is excessive
- Contract dated after credit documents
- Contractis "boiler plate" with limited fill-in-the-blank terms, not reflective of a true negotiation

## Credit Report

- No credit history or "thin" credit files
- Invalid Social Insurance number or variance from that on other documents

- Liabilities shown on credit report that are not on mortgage application
- Length of established credit is not consistent with applicant's age
- Credit patterns are inconsistent with income and lifestyle
- All tradelines opened at the same time
- Significant differences between original and new or supplemental credit reports
- Also Known As (AKA) or Doing Business As (DBA) indicated
- Numerous recent inquiries
- Employment discrepancies

## Appraisal

- Appraisal ordered by a party to the transaction
- Occupant shown to be tenant or unknown
- Owner is someone other than seller shown on sales contract
- Appraisal indicates transaction is a refinance, but other documentation reflects a purchase
- Purchase price is substantially higher than predominant market value
- Purchase price is substantially lower than predominant market value
- Large positive adjustments made to comparable properties
- Comparable sales are not similar in style, size and amenity
- Dated sales used as comparable sales

- New construction / Condo conversion: all comparable sales located in subject development
- Comparable properties are a significant distance from the subject, or located across neighborhood boundaries (main arteries, waterways, etc.)
- Map scale distorts distance of comparable properties
- "For Rent" sign appears in photographs
- Photos appear to be taken from an awkward or unusual standpoint
- Address reflected in photos does not match property address
- Weather conditions in photos inconsistent with average marketing time, date of appraisal
- Appraisal dated before sales contract
- Significant appreciation in short period of time
- Prior sales are listed for subject and/or comparables without adequate explanation

## Title

- Seller not on title
- Seller owned property for short time
- Buyer has pre-existing financial interest in the property
- Date and number of existing encumbrances don't make sense

- Chain of title includes an interested party such as realtor or appraiser
- Buyer and seller have similar names (property flips often use family members as straw buyers)

## Owner Occupancy

## Purchase Transactions:

- Real estate listed on application, yet applicant is a renter
- Applicant intends to lease current residence
- Significant or unrealistic commute distance
- Applicant is downgrading from a larger or more expensive house
- Sales contract is subject to an existing lease
- Occupancy affidavits reflect applicant does *not* intend to occupy
- New homeowner's insurance is a rental policy (declarations page)

## Refinance Transactions:

- Rental property listed on application is more expensive than subject property
- Different mailing address on applicant's bank statements, pay stubs, etc.
- Different address reported on credit report
- Significant or unrealistic commute distance
- Appraisal reflects vacant or tenant occupancy

- Occupancy affidavits reflect applicant does *not* intend to occupy
- Homeowner's insurance is a rental policy (declarations page)
- Reverse directory does not disclose subject property address

# Be Proactive

Yes! Be PROACTIVE rather than REActive in the Mortgage Game

Actively Make sure your trusted broker makes a good presentation of your file; Here is an **example** of mine;

Presenting a solid application from a well financially educated applicant who got caught up in a bit of temporary struggle due to death in the family.
2 years ago the client closed with a private lender and has been making payments regularly.
Client has good equity standing in the property to REFI to a B lender.
What are we looking for?
Client is looking for a B lender 3 years first mortgage 30 years amortization
to pay off the private mortgage after 2 years.
B1 is an internal broker at MCAP and does Cleaning services part time after hour.
B2 is an UBER driver making 60K a year.

Additional incomes are CCB and rental income from live in parents (900/m)
Subject property is owner occupied.

<u>This is a deal, I and the A team got approved at Home Trust. Big relief for the clients.</u>

So be proactive and sum it all up in a story.

By being proactive, you take control of your Finances and will boost your confidence. Being proactive rather than reactive in the mortgage  game can make a significant difference in your real estate investment journey. Here's why:

1. Strategic Planning: Proactive mortgage planning involves looking ahead and developing a comprehensive strategy tailored to your financial goals and investment objectives. By taking the time to understand your borrowing needs, risk tolerance, and long-term plans, you can proactively structure your mortgage financing to align with your investment strategy.

2. Anticipating Challenges: Proactive mortgage planning allows you to anticipate potential challenges and address them before they become significant issues. Whether it's navigating changes in interest rates, adjusting to shifts in the real estate market, or planning for future financing needs, being proactive enables you to stay ahead of the curve and make informed decisions.

3. Accessing Opportunities: By staying proactive, you can position yourself to capitalize on opportunities as they arise in the market. Whether it's securing financing for a lucrative investment property, taking advantage of favorable interest rates, or leveraging equity in your existing properties, proactive mortgage planning empowers you to seize opportunities and maximize your investment potential.

4. Building Relationships: Proactively engaging with mortgage brokers, lenders, and other industry professionals fosters stronger relationships and opens doors to valuable opportunities. By maintaining open lines of communication and staying informed about market trends and lending options, you can build a network of trusted advisors who can

provide guidance and support throughout your real estate investment journey.

5.  Mitigating Risks: Proactive mortgage planning allows you to identify and mitigate potential risks associated with real estate investing. Whether it's conducting thorough due diligence on investment properties, implementing risk management strategies, or diversifying your portfolio, being proactive enables you to protect your investments and minimize potential downside.

Overall, adopting a proactive approach to mortgage planning empowers you to make informed decisions, seize opportunities, and navigate the complexities of real estate investing with confidence. By staying ahead of the curve, anticipating challenges, and leveraging opportunities, you can maximize your investment returns and achieve your financial goals in the mortgage game.

I texted Jim Moelring about whether I should work with a marketing company who cold called me and she said Why you have to be so NOT

**ProActive and react** to these kinds of calls and that was my wake up call to this day. I only work with people that I actively find myself.

# I don't wait to be found.

Thanks Jill.

Part of being active is to improve daily. Join me on my daily Newsletter at HameedAbdi.com/HameedDaily (coming soon)

HOW DO YOU FEEL? AFTER READING THIS BOOK?

INFLUENCED?

EMPOWERED?

Impacted?

Share with others; This a Public service from the A Team and we will appreciate you paying it forward by sharing your perspective.

WE HOPE NOTHING LESS. YOU MATTER. I SEE
YOU, I HEAR AND WORLD WILL LISTEN TO YOU
ONCE YOU MAKE IT TO THE TOP.

LET'S JOURNEY TOGETHER - EMBRACE
EXCELLENCE EVERYDAY. - THE A-TEAM.

www.ingramcontent.com/pod-product-compliance
Lightning Source LLC
Chambersburg PA
CBHW071911210526
45479CB00002B/378

* 9 7 9 8 3 2 9 6 3 3 0 1 6 *